A Travel ✦ Guide to

San Francisco in the 1960s

By James Barter

LUCENT BOOKS®

THOMSON

GALE

San Diego • Detroit • New York • San Francisco • Cleveland • New Haven, Conn. • Waterville, Maine • London • Munich

THOMSON

GALE

Picture Credits:

Cover: Charles E. Rotkin/CORBIS
Associated Press, AP, 50, 51, 56, 61
© Morton Bebe/CORBIS, 42, 65, 78
© Bettmann/CORBIS, 12, 53, 67, 70
© Jan Butchofsky-Houser/CORBIS, 85
© CORBIS, 16, 23, 27
© 1966 CORBIS/Courtesy of NASA/CORBIS,
   23
© Gerald French/CORBIS, 31
© Mark E. Gibson/CORBIS, 17
© Allen Ginsberg/CORBIS, 36, 58
© Lowell Georgia/CORBIS, 79
© Robert Holmes/CORBIS, 14

© Mark A. Johnson/CORBIS, 7
© David Muench/CORBIS, 86
© Roger Ressmeyer/CORBIS, 82
© Royalty free/CORBIS, 30, 88
© Bob Rowan/Progressive Image/CORBIS, 33
© Vincent Stefano/CORBIS, 41
© Joseph Sohm/ChromoSohm Inc./CORBIS,
   63
© Ted Streshinsky/CORBIS, 34, 47, 49, 62, 71,
   83
© Hulton Archive/Getty Images, 18, 19, 37,
   45
Steve Zmina, 8, 39, 46, 55, 57, 60, 68, 74, 75,
   76

For more information, contact
Lucent Books
27500 Drake Rd.
Farmington Hills, MI 48331-3535
Or you can visit our Internet site at http://www.gale.com

LIBRARY OF CONGRESS CATALOGING-IN-PUBLICATION DATA

Barter, James, 1946–
    San Francisco in the 1960s / by James Barter.
        p. cm. — (A travel guide to:)
Summary: A visitor's guide to the history, weather, transportation, overnight
accommodations, dining, shopping, sightseeing, and entertainment of San Francisco
in 1967.
    ISBN 1-59018-359-2 (alk. paper)
    1. San Francisco (Calif.)—History—20th century—Juvenile literature. 2. San Francisco
(CA)—Social life and customs—20th century—Juvenile literature. 3. Nineteen
sixties—Juvenile literature. 4. San Francisco (Calif.)—Guidebooks—Juvenile literature.
[1. San Francisco (Calif.)—History—20th century. 2. San Francisco (Calif.)—Social life and
customs—20th century. 3. San Francisco (Calif.)—Description and travel.] I. Title.
II. Travel guide (Lucent Books).
    F869.S357B47 2004
    9779.4'61'09046—dc22
                                                                2003015071

Contents

Foreword

Travel can be a unique way to learn about oneself and other cultures. The esteemed American writer and historian, John Hope Franklin, poetically expressed his conviction in the value of travel by urging, "We must go beyond textbooks, go out into the bypaths and untrodden depths of the wilderness and travel and explore and tell the world the glories of our journey." The message communicated by this eloquent entreaty is clear: The value of travel is to temper one's imagination about a place and its people with reality, and instead of thinking how things may be, to be able to experience them as they really are.

Franklin's voice is not alone in his summons for students to "travel and explore." He is joined by a stentorian chorus of thinkers that includes former president John F. Kennedy, who established the Peace Corps to facilitate cross-cultural understandings between Americans and citizens of other lands. Ideas about the benefits of travel do not spring only from contemporary times. The ancient Greek historian Herodotus journeyed to foreign lands for the purpose of immersing himself in unfamiliar cultural traditions. In this way, he believed, he might gain a firsthand understanding of people and ways of life in other places.

The joys, insights, and satisfaction that travelers derive from their journeys are not limited to cultural understanding. Travel has the added value of enhancing the traveler's inner self by expanding his or her range of experiences. Writer Paul Tournier concurs that, "The real meaning of travel, like that of a conversation by the fireside, is the discovery of oneself through contact with other people."

The Lucent Books Travel Guide series enlivens history by introducing a new and innovative style and format. Each volume in the series presents the history of a preeminent historical travel destination written in the casual style and format of a travel guide. Whether providing a tour of fifth-century B.C. Athens, Renaissance Florence, or Shakespeare's London, each book describes a city or area at its cultural peak and orients readers to only those places and activities that are known to have existed at that time.

A high level of authenticity is achieved in the Travel Guide series. Each book is written in the present tense and addresses the reader as a prospective foreign traveler. The sense of authenticity is further achieved, whenever possible, by the inclusion of descriptive quotations by contemporary writers who knew the place; information on fascinating historical sites; and travel tips meant to explain unusual cultural idiosyncrasies that give depth and texture to all great cultural centers. Even shopping details, such as where to buy an ermine-trimmed gown, or a much-needed house slave, are included to inform readers of what items were sought after throughout history.

Looked at collectively, this series presents an appealing presentation of many of the cultural and social highlights of Western civilization. The collection also provides a framework for discussion about the larger historical currents that dominated not only each travel destination but countries and entire continents as well. Each book is customized by the author to bring to the fore the most important and most interesting characteristics that define each title. High standards of scholarship are assured in the series by the generous peppering of relevant quotes and extensive bibliographies. These tools provide readers a scholastic standard for their own research as well as a guide to direct them to other books, periodicals, and websites that will provide them greater breadth and detail.

The City

Whether living in trendy Marin County just north across the Golden Gate Bridge, in the East Bay university town of Berkeley, in blue-collar Oakland, or in the heart of San Francisco itself, everyone refers to this splendid cosmopolitan jewel as "the city." Loved passionately by residents and nonresidents alike, San Francisco is ranked as America's most popular vacation destination on the West Coast and is consistently rated America's most picturesque, sophisticated city.

Today, in 1967, San Franciscans can look back and understand that the city's attraction is not accidental. San Francisco's geography is the envy of the world. Part of the city's natural beauty is its forty or so hills that shape the landscape, providing residents and travelers with long, dramatic vistas from hill to hill, across the city, and down to the bay.

Dotted with a handful of islands, the San Francisco Bay flows north and south and wraps itself around San Francisco, providing the city with one of the world's great natural harbors. The Golden Gate, a 1.2-mile-wide gap in the coastal mountain range, acts as a great watery portal, allowing water from the Pacific Ocean to fill the bay. Fog has given San Francisco one of its nicknames, Fog City, and earthquakes have given rise to San Francisco's other nickname, Quake City.

Yet geography alone cannot explain San Francisco's magnetism. For the past one hundred years or so, San Franciscans have been hard at work embellishing their city's natural beauty. By far the most beautiful, beloved, and identifiable addition is the Golden Gate Bridge. This mile-long, gold-colored, steel span is universally recognized as a rare feat of human engineering that has enhanced nature's pristine beauty. Another gem of engineering that artfully defines San Francisco is its fleet of fabled cable cars. Rolling on rails while pulled along by an underground cable, these diminutive wooden cars glide up and down the city's steepest streets clanging their bells.

There is still more to San Francisco than the wonders of geography and engineering; there are its neighborhoods. The city is famous for these neighborhoods that lend a rhythm and vibrancy rarely found elsewhere. Chinatown, the largest enclave of Chinese outside of Asia, is filled with the chatter of several Chinese dialects.

North Beach, the sprawling Italian neighborhood, is filled with the smells of marinara and sausages sold for lunch and dinner at sidewalk cafés. At Fisherman's Wharf fishing boats still unload their catches of fish and crabs that can then be eaten freshly cooked at any number of wharf-side restaurants with commanding views of the Golden Gate Bridge and Alcatraz Island. Bakeries at the wharf produce the best sourdough bread outside of Paris.

Other neighborhoods are filled with row after row of colorful Victorian homes. Living in these neighborhoods, although not in the finer homes, are the beat writers and poets who hang out in North

Fog settles over San Francisco's Golden Gate Bridge, one of the city's most recognizable landmarks.

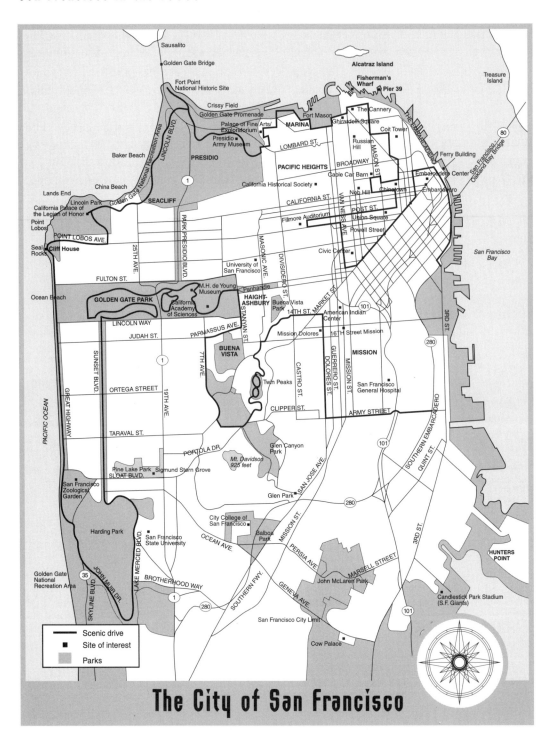

The City of San Francisco

Beach cafés; and not far away in the Haight-Ashbury district live the colorful and flamboyant free-spirited hippies.

Be aware that many people plan only a short visit yet end up falling in love with the city and never go home. Writer Inez Hayes Irwin said about her experience following a short visit here: "You could live in San Francisco a month and ask no greater entertainment than simply walking through it."[1] But for native San Franciscans, the compliment that best reflects their love for the city was uttered by Herb Caen, columnist for the *San Francisco Chronicle*, who once said: "One day if I do go to heaven, I'll look around and say, 'It ain't bad, but it ain't San Francisco.'"[2]

Chapter 1

The History of San Francisco

According to anthropologists, the earliest Native Americans arrived here about fifteen thousand years ago. Their arrival coincided with the melting of massive sheets of glacial ice covering this entire region that signaled the end of the last great Ice Age.

The American Indian tribes that moved in as the ice melted were the Coastal Miwok and Ohlone who inhabited the hills circling the San Francisco Bay and a few of the larger islands in the bay. These Native Americans fished the waters for shark, striped bass, and crab while collecting bird eggs near marshes along the bay's edge. They hunted the plentiful deer that bounded through the hills of thickly wooded oak forests and foraged for the vegetables and nuts that grew plentifully on the verdant rolling hills in this temperate climate.

Living in a region with neither intense winter cold nor sweltering summer heat, the American Indians lived in conical-shaped structures called *umachas* covered with thick strips of bark and a second layer of pine-tree branches and needles to shed the rain. Along the bottom three feet of the *umachas* an outer layer of dirt and mud was piled against the branches to strengthen the structure. Inside each *umacha* was a space to store acorn flour, beds made of pine needles covered with animal hides, and an open fire pit for cooking and for warming the home during the winter.

This relatively simple and self-sustaining lifestyle remained little changed for several thousand years until the late sixteenth century. At that time several European nations, spearheaded by England, Spain, and Italy, sent out explorers to learn more about the world and its valuable natural resources. Most of all explorers sought to circumnavigate the globe for the first time, establish trading partnerships with Asian nations, and return to Europe with their ships' holds loaded with gold, spices, and other valuables.

The Arrival of Europeans

The first European visitors to the San Francisco Bay completely missed the Golden Gate inlet. In 1579 Sir Francis Drake landed at Point Reyes, about thirty miles north of San Francisco. He went ashore and erected a bronze plaque claiming the region for Queen Elizabeth of England and then sailed right past the Golden Gate on his way south without discovering the bay. Most historians speculate that fog probably shrouded the gate on that day.

Almost two hundred years passed until the Spanish, who were exploring and conquering Mexico, sent both land and sea expeditions to explore and secure California. Rumors about the existence of the San Francisco Bay had filtered to them from American Indian tribes living here. A land expedition led by Gaspar de Portolá began 450 miles to the south in San Diego, California, and headed north until discovering San Francisco Bay on November 2, 1769.

One of Portolá's men, Miguel Costansó, recorded this event in his diary:

> Several of the soldiers requested permission to go hunting. . . . From the columns of smoke they had noticed all over the level country, there was no doubt that the land must be well populated with natives. This ought to confirm us more and more in the opinion that we were at the port of San Francisco.[3]

Six years following Portolá's discovery, the Spanish frigate, *San Carlos*, under the command of Juan Manuel de Ayala, made the first recorded entry into San Francisco Bay through the Golden Gate on August 5, 1775. Ayala scouted the bay for six weeks, charting its geographical characteristics and noting its desirability as a natural port.

For the next forty-five years, Spain controlled San Francisco Bay until Mexico revolted and drove the Spanish out of California. Although few white Americans settled and traveled through the West in the early nineteenth century, a small number were beginning to discover Texas, Oregon, Washington, and northern California. It did not take long for the interests of American settlers to collide with the interests of the Mexicans.

In June 1846 skirmishes between American pioneers and Mexican troops prompted the United States to declare

Gaspar de Portolá and his men discover San Francisco Bay in 1769. Portolá's expedition reached San Francisco after traveling 450 miles from San Diego.

war on Mexico. A group of renegade American settlers led by Kit Carson and John C. Frémont attacked and seized the Mexican garrison in Sonoma, forty miles north of San Francisco. They declared California independent from Mexico and named it the California Republic. Emboldened by their success, they took their rebellion to San Francisco, where they attacked and took over the Mexican fort. On May 30, 1848, the war ended with Mexico's surrender, and all of California came under the control of the United States.

The Discovery of Gold

Unperturbed by a brief war taking place far away, John Sutter was building a sawmill in the small town of Colma a hundred miles northeast of San Francisco in the foothills of the Sierra Nevada mountain range. One day in January 1848 Sutter's foreman, Jim Marshall, came to his work shed with a handkerchief stuffed in his pocket, insisting that Sutter immediately lock the door so he could reveal the secret hidden within the handkerchief. Bewildered by the odd request, Sutter initially refused and then explained in his memoirs what happened next:

> Marshall took a rag from his pocket, showing me the yellow metal: he had about two ounces of it. . . . After having proved the metal with aqua fortis [an acid used to test gold], which I found in my apothecary shop, likewise with other ex-

periments, and read the long article "gold" in the *Encyclopedia Americana*, I declared this to be gold of the finest quality, of at least 23 carats.[4]

Keeping the discovery of gold a secret proved to be impossible, and word of the initial discovery and many subsequent discoveries spread down the Sierra foothills to San Francisco. Within weeks a frenzy of gold fever swept the San Francisco Bay area. Men with no mining experience packed horses and mules and headed to the foothills with unrealistic fantasies of striking it rich. Despite miserable disappointment for most miners, strikes on a few rich veins of gold created headlines.

By 1849 reports of gold had spread throughout America and the rest of the world. Ships loaded with optimistic prospectors bound for the Sierras sailed for San Francisco, the closest port to the gold fields. In little more than a year, the population of San Francisco exploded. Bay Area historian John Martini makes this observation about the gold rush of 1849 and the miners, dubbed the "forty-niners," who flocked here: "San Francisco seeming grew overnight from a village of 300 people to a metropolis of 35,000. California became the focal point of world attention, and the little-used bay was suddenly, incalculably, valuable."[5]

By 1859 the initial gold-rush fever had cooled. The mining fever flared again in the early 1860s, but this time the rush was for silver in an area called the Comstock Lode near Reno, Nevada. Within a few years gold and silver rushes dried up, but the construction of the transcontinental railroad through California and Nevada provided work for many and continued to fuel the growth of San Francisco once it was linked by rail with the East Coast.

Post–Gold Rush

By the turn of the century San Francisco's population had grown by a factor of ten to almost 350,000, the biggest city west of Chicago. The Klondike gold rush in Canada's Yukon in 1896 and the Spanish-American War in 1898 placed further demands on San Francisco as the only reliable West Coast port where goods and troops could be stockpiled and dispersed. Both events underscored the city's importance as a port, while the opening of numerous banks, insurance companies, railroad terminals, and shipyards established San Francisco's continuing importance as a financial and industrial center.

Gold was discovered at John Sutter's sawmill in January of 1848. The discovery brought hundreds of thousands of gold seekers to the San Francisco Bay area.

Then the earthquake of 1906 stuck. On April 18, at 5:13 in the morning, San Francisco experienced the worst earthquake in the nation's history. Fire broke out shortly after the earthquake, and by nine o'clock much of the city was engulfed in flames that leaped quickly from block to block. Water pressure to the fire hoses was too low to douse the flames, and fire departments were able to do little more than wait for the fire to burn itself out. San Francisco was devastated more by the ensuing firestorm than by the earthquake itself. One

San Francisco and the Forty-Niners

No single event in the history of San Francisco was of greater consequence than the discovery of gold in 1848. By the start of 1849, word of the discovery had spread to the East Coast, Europe, and as far away as China. Hundreds of thousands of gold seekers—nicknamed the forty-niners—speaking dozens of languages arrived in San Francisco by boat to join the rush. Sailing ships littered the docks to such an extent that many had to anchor in the bay to unload passengers and cargo because there was no room at the docks.

San Francisco profited more from the gold rush than did the miners. Ready to greet these men were San Francisco merchants, some of whom charged inflated prices for supplies and housing. Newspapers from this era record businessmen buying up every mining tool and commodity such as shovels, mining pans, picks, horses, food, and clothing. After they had cornered the market, they raised prices dramatically, forcing newly arrived miners to pay up to fifteen dollars for a mining pan that the merchants had bought for just fifty cents a few weeks earlier.

With their millions made from the forty-niners, merchants such as jeans manufacturer Levi Strauss, sugar magnate John D. Spreckels, and coffee tycoon James Folger, greatly contributed to the city's cultural and financial reputation.

eyewitness, Charles B. Sedgwick, wrote in his journal:

Buildings were entirely gone, while the colossal City Hall, the principal edifice of the town, was a hopeless, pitiful wreck; its mighty walls rent; its once beautiful rotunda a great gaping wound; its huge dome supported by nothing but a gaunt skeleton of empty framework. In the side streets the havoc was as bad; in places vastly worse. On O'Farrell many structures had fallen; the entire front wall of Delmonico's had dropped away, leaving the upper rooms exposed to view. Whole floors had been broken up, stairways had collapsed, marble facings torn away. And in the rear of this, south of Market street, a great sea of flame was steadily rolling forward with a dull hungry roar, relieved only by the still louder roar of failing buildings at frequent intervals, and thunderous earsplitting explosions when dynamite was used in the vain effort to check the fiery advance. A changed San Francisco, indeed, from the secure, care-free, luxurious place of the day before![6]

Modern San Francisco

Following the worst devastation in the city's history, San Franciscans pulled together to rebuild. Within five years all of the rubble had been removed and a far more modern city emerged. The new city and the opening of the Panama Canal, an achievement that greatly improved San Francisco's shipping interests were celebrated at the World's Fair here in 1915 naming the celebration the Panama-Pacific Exposition. Two decades later, as the population continued to surge, two of the most prominent landmarks in the Bay Area—the San Francisco–Oakland Bay

Only the shells of buildings remain on this hillside after the 1906 San Francisco earthquake. The earthquake and subsequent fires destroyed much of the city.

Mission Dolores

On the corner of Dolores and Sixteenth Streets is San Francisco's oldest historical monument, Mission Dolores. Founded in June 1776 this white stucco church is also the oldest building in the city. It is also the only intact mission chapel in the chain of twenty-one missions established in California under the direction of Father Serra that began in San Diego and ended twenty miles north of San Francisco in Sonoma. The purpose of Serra's chain of missions was twofold: It introduced Christianity to Native American tribes and provided headquarters for Spanish soldiers who established firm control over the land and the American Indian population for the king of Spain.

As visitors approach the heavy wooden entry doors, each will realize that the mission is built like a fort, with heavy oak doors, few windows, a rock foundation extending four feet below the surface, and ten-foot-thick adobe walls. The entry facade incorporates four huge columns supporting a second-story balcony housing an additional six smaller columns and three signal bells. Architectural historians estimate the number of adobe blocks in the missions's walls to be thirty-six thousand. Just to the left of the entry courtyard is a fascinating cemetery for some five thousand American Indians, as well as many notable early San Franciscans.

Founded in 1776, Mission Dolores is San Francisco's oldest historical monument.

17

The 1906 Earthquake

The most dramatic natural disaster in the history of San Francisco occurred at 5:13 A.M. on April 18, 1906. Just before sunrise that Wednesday morning, the San Andreas Fault, a deep fissure in the earth's crust that runs just a few miles east of San Francisco, suddenly shifted.

When the earthquake struck, hundreds of buildings in the downtown area partially or entirely collapsed. Fires erupted throughout the city and by mid-morning crowds of citizens escaped to the tops of hills and witnessed the devastation and horror of the city engulfed in flames. Water pressure to the fire hoses was too low to douse the flames, forcing the fire department to do little more than wait for the fire to burn itself out. By nightfall, three hundred thousand San Franciscans were homeless.

Also of concern to the citizenry and the chief of police was the scourge of looters. E.E. Schmitz, mayor of San Francisco at the time, issued this proclamation: "The Federal Troops, the members of the regular police force and all special police officers have

A shift in the San Andreas Fault caused San Francisco's catastrophic 1906 earthquake.

been authorized by me to KILL any and all persons found engaged in looting or the commission of any other crime."

Within weeks of the disaster, San Franciscans quickly recovered, cleared the rubble, and began replacing many of the collapsed buildings with new and more beautiful ones still in use today.

Bridge and the Golden Gate Bridge—were completed in 1936 and 1937 respectively. They remain to this day, thirty years later, the most magnificent symbols of San Francisco.

Following the Japanese attack on Pearl Harbor in December 1941 signaling America's entry into World War II, San Francisco and other Bay Area ports became the leaders in West Coast shipbuilding operations. The demand for steel manufacturers, welders, pipe fitters, engine designers, and steel-assembly workers witnessed the largest influx of population since the gold rush. The Bay Area, with its gigantic shipyards, became a major launching pad for military operations in the Pacific. When the war ended in 1945, many returning soldiers and sailors stayed in San Francisco, and the city experienced yet another economic and population boost.

In the mid-1950s national attention was again focused on "The City by the Bay" as the birthplace of the beat generation when writers Jack Kerouac, Allen Ginsberg, and Gregory Corso departed New York City and joined forces with a San Francisco poets' movement begun by poet and literary critic Kenneth Rexroth and his friends Gary Snyder and Philip Whalen. As these writers and poets gained national notoriety speaking for the politically and socially alienated, they gained a significant footing in literary America and quickly became widely read and regarded as one of the most significant American literary groups in fifty years. Most of the beat writers gravitated to the North Beach area of San Francisco

In recent decades, San Francisco has grown and prospered. Today, the city is a thriving urban area with a large and diverse population.

The Bay

The growth of San Francisco would not have occurred had it not been for the bay. During the early twentieth century, the growth of downtown San Francisco and construction of the first two great bridges depended upon the bay for delivery of construction materials.

The West Coast had no mills to produce the tons of steel needed to construct skyscrapers and bridges. To build these major engineering projects, steel was made and formed on the East Coast, loaded on ships, and transported through the Panama Canal and up the West Coast to San Francisco Bay. The prime example of this process was the construction of the Golden Gate Bridge. When the bridge was built in the 1930s, the 88,000 tons of steel I-beams for its twin towers and the 61,500 tons of steel cables were fabricated in Pennsylvania and shipped to San Francisco on freighters. Without the bay, the steel for such a colossal effort could not have been delivered.

The Golden Gate Bridge as seen at night.

near City Lights Books bookstore where their works were sold when other mainstream bookstores refused to carry their works.

Now, roughly ten years later, the beat writers are being joined by a more recent movement labeled by the media as the hippie generation. These younger participants are drawn together by music rather than literature and are characterized by a multitude of political and social convictions. Leading the current list are the anti–Vietnam War movement, the civil rights movement, the recent hallucinogenic-drug revolution, and the sexual revolution. The hippies, loosely estimated to number about twenty thousand, have gravitated to the Haight-Ashbury section of the city near Golden Gate Park.

This summer is already being described as the Summer of Love by local newspapers, and planned activities are expected to draw thousands of free spirits to enjoy a summer of free rock-and-roll music, dancing, friendship, and general frivolity throughout the streets of San Francisco.

Chapter 2

Location, Weather, and Arrival

San Francisco is located on California's Pacific coast. It is the largest city in this half of the state. San Francisco's geographic area is surprisingly small considering its large international reputation. About 750,000 residents live on the forty-six-square-mile tip of the San Francisco peninsula that is surrounded on three sides by the San Francisco Bay and the Pacific Ocean. The population density averages 16,300 persons per square mile.

The geography of this northern California region has assisted the city in finding extra room. This region is one of America's most active seismic zones and has a long history of earthquakes and tectonic plate activity that have combined to push up San Francisco's surface to create dozens of hills. Each hill provides additional sloping surface area on which entire neighborhoods and city landmarks have

been built. Although this same seismic activity has been responsible for toppling buildings and houses from time to time, the city has not suffered a major earthquake since 1906. San Franciscans remain remarkably upbeat about earthquakes: Although everyone candidly knows that the next "big one" will inevitably occur, no one knows when.

In some respects the history of earthquakes has conspired to make San Francisco a safer city compared to cities outside earthquake zones. Structural engineers in San Francisco are constructing the world's safest skyscrapers because they understand that all buildings must be able to sustain the impact of a major quake. This awareness forces them to build to the most rigorous standards. Two of the structural innovations invented here that are now used around the world are soft foundations and safety glass. Large building foundations are built to shift slightly in a quake rather than stand rigid. This innovation prevents the steel from snapping and toppling tall structures. The glass used in large windows is laminated safety glass that will shatter into thousands of small pieces if it pops out during an earthquake rather than remain intact and sail down in huge sheets on unsuspecting pedestrians.

The San Francisco Bay

Once travelers arrive here, each quickly understands that San Francisco is a gift of the bay. Without the bay San Francisco would be little more than another of the several ordinary cities sprinkled along California's eight-hundred-mile coastline. Or it might not have become a city at all. Satellite photographs of the San Francisco Bay area reveal to modern viewers the significance of the bay to eighteenth-century explorers and sailors as a safe, natural harbor where captains of small wooden sailing ships could escape the treacherous high seas of the Pacific. Once the Spanish discovered the bay, sailors flocked here confident of finding a safe landing place to rest their crews and replenish their supplies.

Three hundred years later the bay remains the heart and soul of San Francisco. Today modern international steel freighters and con-tainer ships continue to sail through the Golden Gate daily, seeking the safety of wharves to unload their products. Their cargoes, crews, and cultural influences sustain San Francisco's reputation as one of the world's major international ports. The number of foreign languages heard in the wharf area is one of many indicators of San Francisco's international importance.

This satellite picture shows the San Francisco Bay area. The bay provided eighteenth-century sailors with a safe, natural harbor.

Besides commercial shipping the Bay Area is the home of several U.S. naval bases. Because of the importance of the bay as a port for large military ships, the height of Golden Gate Bridge was determined in order to accommodate aircraft carriers, the tallest ships in the world. The bay is also home to thousands of amateur sailors who strap on their foul-weather gear to challenge the bay in their sailboats. When the weather is sunny and the winds brisk, the sailboats colorful, billowing sails leaning into the wind scatter across the bay between the Golden Gate and the Berkeley yacht harbor.

Fortunately for everyone the weather in San Francisco is both more enjoyable and more predictable than earthquakes. For visitors from the Northwest, San Francisco's weather will provide many more sunny days, and for guests from the East and Midwest, the city's climate will be far more agreeable than what they can expect back home.

Climate

San Francisco's year-round temperate climate is the envy of nearly every major American city. Blessed with a location that precludes winter snows and summer's sweltering humidity, San Francisco is a vacationer's paradise that can be enjoyed 365 days a year. The Pacific Ocean cur-rents act as an insulation barrier in the winter because their waters are warmer than the air temperature. During the summer their waters are cooler than the air. As the air and water temperatures combine, they modify each other—to the delight of San Franciscans.

San Francisco's temperate climate creates two distinct seasons. The rainy season begins in November and runs through April. During these six months rainfall averages eighteen inches. During the other six months the average drops to a mere three inches. Temperatures tend to follow this pattern, with the winter months averaging highs in the high fifty and low sixty degrees Fahrenheit, and summer highs averaging in the high sixty and low seventy degrees Fahrenheit. From time to time winter temperatures may drop into the forties for a day or two or soar into the nineties during the summer, but these extremes are infrequent and do not disrupt the flow of the city.

The one climatic characteristic everyone associates with San Francisco is its fog. Fog can develop any time of the year but is primarily a summer phenomenon. In the evenings a blanket of fog may wrap itself around the city, but by ten o'clock the next morning it gives way to bright sunlight until about six or seven o'clock, when it returns and settles in for the night.

San Francisco Fog

San Franciscans take their fog seriously. Beginning in the early summer, great billowy fog banks wrap themselves around San Francisco. The shrouding begins with the twin spires of the Golden Gate Bridge, then Coit Tower, and eventually the entire city. Some impertinent San Franciscans have adopted the attitude that until a person knows and enjoys the fog, he or she cannot not know and enjoy San Francisco.

In this city of exuberant urban pride, the fog is an integral part of its mystique. This is the only place on Earth where the residents are able to distinguish between fog banks, fog fronts, fog eddies, fog domes, fog surges, fog wreaths, fog cascades, and fog falls. This is also the place with the radio station KFOG, the Fog City Diner, Fog Bar and Grill, Fog Publishing House, and Old Foghorn beer.

Perhaps the city's bakers, famed for their San Francisco sourdough bread, carry the air of mystery about the fog the furthest. They claim that the reason their bread cannot be reproduced outside of San Francisco is because the particular yeast mold used in the baking process thrives in the foggy air in a way that cannot be reproduced elsewhere.

Unlike most cities, here the fog is one of the most loved elements.

The real secret of San Francisco weather is that the very best month for warm, clear weather is October. Although this may be hard to believe, meteorologists who specialize in weather analysis explain this phenomenon that is a result of temperature changes in the ocean, the inland valley several miles east of San Francisco, and the air of the jet stream at an altitude of thirty thousand feet.

Getting Here

Since the demise of ocean-liner travel two decades ago, visitors coming to San Francisco are now limited to air, train, and car travel. The train however, cannot transverse any of the bridges, so tourists must still rely on a car to take them into the city. Of the three modes of travel, the most interesting and scenic is by car, but the best way to get your bearings in San Francisco and the surrounding Bay Area is to arrive by plane.

Flying into the city on a clear day allows you to locate many of the area landmarks you will want to visit later. Far below you, as your plane circles into either San Francisco or Oakland airports, you will be able to spot the bay and its three major bridges that link the communities on its periphery. On the eastern edge of the bay is the Golden Gate Bridge. The San Francisco–Oakland Bay Bridge passes across Yerba Buena Island connecting the east bay with San Francisco. The Richmond–San Rafael Bridge links the northern bay cities of Richmond and San Rafael.

Dotting the bay below is a handful of islands, and your flight in gives you a good geographic overview of the layout of the city and its surrounding area. The largest island is Angel Island, a great hiking and picnic area worth visiting.

The *Oracle*

One way to learn about and to understand the hippie psychedelic movement that recently emerged in San Francisco is to stop at any newsstand or bookstore and purchase a copy of San Francisco's counterculture weekly newspaper, the *San Francisco Oracle*. The *Oracle*, with its trademark artistic and flamboyant psychedelic cover, is ten to twelve pages containing an assortment of poems by San Francisco's beat poets, interviews with Bay Area intellectuals, honest and informative articles about psychedelic drug use, where to find free food and housing, editorials opposing the Vietnam War, and music reviews of local bands.

The first issue of the *Oracle* was published in 1966 by Allen Cohen, who lives in the Haight-Ashbury community. According to cultural historian George Riser in an interview with Cohen, the *Oracle*'s goal is "To confront its readers with a rainbow of beauty and words ringing with truth and transcendence." The quality of the writing, the modern forward-thinking articles, and the respected gurus of the hippie counterculture make the paper a success. The paper claims 125,000 paying customers and five times that number who read it without paying for it; if people do not have the money for the paper, Cohen lets them take it for free.

One way of attempting to understand what the *Oracle* means to the San Francisco hippie subculture was recently expressed by Cohen, who had this to say using typical 1960s jargon employing language, metaphors, and mysticism:

So, looking at an *Oracle* could be a sort of occult trance experience communicated across the dimensions of space and time, through the tabloid medium, from one explorer of inner worlds to another. That was the magic, the fire, that spread from mind to mind with the *Oracle*. Motifs and techniques were universal—from ancient Chinese spirals to Sci Fi. Wings, rays, auras, arabesques, swirls, unicorns, and centaurs, mandalas, collages, flying saucers and their inhabitants, op-art, flowers and paisley, nudes, feathers, and ghosted images were interwoven into a dazzling cross-cultural spectacle of multidimensional depth, pattern and flow.

The smaller island, just to the south, is far more well known but one you cannot visit; this is Alcatraz, the onetime federal penitentiary. The island through which the San Francisco–Oakland Bay Bridge passes, Yerba Buena, is used as a small naval base that has secondary value for fishermen after crab and local fish.

Before your plane lands try to spot a few more of the other Bay Area's landmarks so you can visit them later. The most prominent on the east bay is the three-hundred-foot bell tower on the campus of the University of California in Berkeley; on the coast north of the bay is Mount Tamalpais; and the fifty-story Bank of America building in the heart of San

Francisco's downtown financial district is the tallest building on the West Coast.

Should you land at night the view is perhaps even more spectacular. All of the cities on the perimeter of the bay are lit up in stark contrast to the bay's dark water. Each of San Francisco's skyscrapers that collectively define the downtown area creates a visual pulse of energy illuminating the night sky. Added to their light show are the lights on the three bridges that create the impression of strings of jewelry linking three sides of the bay. A favorite of all San Franciscans is the view on foggy nights of the revolving red beacons on the top of each spire of the Golden Gate Bridge. The lights shine their beams across the horizon warning away aircraft.

Driving

The most enjoyable way to drive to San Francisco is to head over to Highway 1, the scenic stretch of road that hugs the dramatic Pacific coastline. Vacationers coming from the East Coast can link up with Highway 1 at several points south of the city to enjoy the picturesque drive north, and those coming from Los Angeles can catch the famous route north of Santa Barbara.

From Santa Barbara north, mile after mile of Highway 1 presents drivers with views of the most beautiful coastal areas blessed with dramatic views of the surf crashing against towering and rugged cliffs. This stretch of asphalt also weaves through natural habitats of redwood forests, coastal mountain ranges, and national parks.

As the highway passes by the city of San Simeon, travelers will enjoy stopping for a paid tour of Hearst Castle, newspaper entrepreneur William Randolph Hearst's lavish residence built during the 1920s. Hearst Castle is a ninety-thousand-square-foot palace overlooking the Pacific that contains fifty-six bedrooms, forty-one fireplaces, and several indoor and outdoor swimming pools. After Hearst's death in 1951, his castle became a state monument and is one of the most popular tourist attractions in southern California.

Sixty-five miles north of San Simeon is the coastal community of Big Sur. From beaches to mountains, vacationers can stop and hike along the streams

Expansive ocean vistas are just one of the many attractions that make traveling Highway 1 through Big Sur a driver's delight.

The rocky coast of Monterey is just one of many beautiful spots drivers can visit on their way to San Francisco.

in the cool tree-lined valleys and climb up on the high ridges for a spectacular view of the coastline on the western slope. Big Sur is a hiker's paradise and occasional home to many American writers such as Henry Miller, John Steinbeck, and Robinson Jeffers.

Forty miles north the highway leads to Carmel and Monterey, two of the oldest historical sites and most photographed coastal communities in northern Califor-

nia. Each is known for its windswept coastline, offshore protected habitat for seals, sea lions, and sea otters, and temperate climate. For art lovers each town boasts dozens of fine galleries. These towns were the settings for many of John Steinbeck's award-winning novels.

From here the remainder of the drive to San Francisco will take travelers through the thickly wooded Santa Cruz Mountains into the city.

Chapter 3

First Day, Getting to Know the City

San Francisco is a city of neighborhoods. Each is rich in culture with its own distinctive charm and character. Some rise high among the flatlands, their hilltop bluffs peppering the landscape with spots for unparalleled panoramic views and an interesting mix of unique experiences. Others hug the city's coastline and docks, providing San Francisco with its signature Golden Gate Bridge, Fisherman's Wharf, views of the San Francisco Bay, and western-facing beaches of the Pacific Ocean. Still others flow out across the city's flatlands. A little north of downtown are Chinatown, North Beach, and Russian Hill, each of which provides a dazzling mix of foreign languages and exotic foods. A little to the west are Haight-Ashbury, Golden Gate Park, Pacific Heights, Lincoln Park, and the Pre-

sidio, each of which is deserving of a visit for anyone interested in enjoying and understanding the city.

Finding Your Way Around

A car is the last thing you want in San Francisco. Exploring San Francisco by car involves navigating a maze of one-way streets, freeway interchanges, bridge toll booths, and restricted parking zones. San Francisco's famed forty or more hills, some of which present a 30 percent grade, can be an additional terrifying problem for drivers who are accustomed to driving on flat terrain. Some hills are so steep that the city engineers score the concrete for better tire traction. Perhaps worst of all for drivers is the hunt for a parking place once you have reached a destination for the day. The city's shortage of street parking spaces forces many to pay daily parking lot fees that can cost as much as a dinner for two. Instead why not think about abandoning your car in favor of public transportation and the pleasure of walking or bicycling the city?

For visitors who enjoy brisk walks, San Francisco is a walker's paradise. Most of the city's key attractions are located within the compact location that resembles a slice of pie. This slice of the city is bounded by Van Ness Avenue and Market Street forming the two sides, and the Embarcadero, the round edge of the pie. This section is home to the classy shops around Union Square, Chinatown, swanky Nob Hill and Russian Hill, bohemian North Beach with its Telegraph Hill, and the epicenter of tourism, Fisherman's Wharf. All of

Cable cars are San Francisco's most famous form of public transportation.

these spots are within easy walking distance, and much of the enjoyment of the walks is the spectacular view of the city and the bay as you trek up and down the many picturesque hills.

San Francisco also provides several forms of public transport that are inexpensive yet efficient. Cable cars, buses, and trolleys can take you to or near every major attraction for less than one dollar in each direction. Ferries have enjoyed a modest revival in recent years, and they provide services from Fisherman's Wharf and the Embarcadero to Alameda, Oakland, Sausalito, Tiburon, and the bay islands. The next time you visit San Francisco, the city will have completed its newest transportation system, the Bay Area Rapid Transit system—BART for short. This is a subway system that will soon connect multiple San Francisco locations with the suburbs.

Cable Cars

Cable cars are a San Francisco invention. They are the city's most famous form of public transportation and most endearing symbol. They remain one of a handful of moving national historic landmarks. These throwbacks to an earlier time are an exhilarating way to ride up and down San Francisco hills. Their fame comes from their combination of practical, reliable transportation coupled with a dash of fun.

The Cable Car Barn

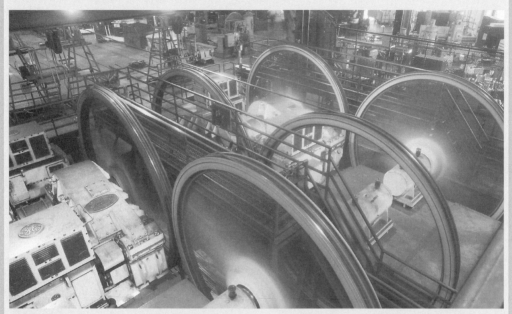

The cables that run the city's cable cars are powered here, inside the Cable Car Barn and Powerhouse.

If you have been bitten by the cable car "bug" and want to learn all there is to know about these little cars that contribute to San Francisco's magical mystique, wander over to the corner of Mason and Washington Streets where you will find the Cable Car Barn and Powerhouse. This is where the cable cars are housed, repaired, and where the cables under the streets are powered.

Each of the three separate cable-car lines is powered by a one-and-five-eighths-inch steel cable running under the streets moving at a constant nine-and-a-half miles per hour. The three enormous drive wheels can be seen turning at the barn. Unlike most types of trains and trolleys that have motors, cable cars move on rails using a gripping device similar to a large pair of pliers. To attach to and detach from the moving underground cable, the gripman pulls or pushes on a lever that connects the gripping device to the cable. When the cars head down steep hills, the gripman releases the cable and lets the car coast. On level ground and going up hills, the gripman pulls back the lever and attaches to the cable. To stop the car the gripman releases the cable and the brakeman applies the brakes. The distinctive clanging of the two bells mounted on each car are used to signal starting and stopping between the gripman up front and the brakeman on the back.

Just thirty feet long, eight feet wide, and ten feet high, these bite-sized cars ride on three-and-a-half-foot-wide steel rails. Each can seat twenty-nine passengers and carry an additional thirty-one standing up and a crew of two. Mobs of riders stand on the wooden running boards on the outsides of the cable car and must hang on to keep from falling off. One of the unique thrills of riding one is being able to watch the engineer who operates the car, called the gripman. Standing in the midst of riders, the gripman pulls and pushes on a lever that connects and disconnects the car from the cable running under the street. The brakeman riding in the back applies the brakes. Always in good spirits the gripman and brakeman put on a show for tourists that includes the ringing of the distinctive cable car bells that signal each other back and forth when to start and stop.

San Francisco has three cable-car lines carrying passengers throughout the heart of the tourist area. The cars on each line are painted the specific line colors so they can be easily identified from a distance. Part of the fun is waiting for the car to approach and then jumping on the moment it stops to load and unload passengers. The cars are always packed, so do not be squeamish about piling on.

Ferryboats

Another of San Francisco's unusual modes of transportation not often seen elsewhere is the ferryboat fleet that still plies the bay. The number of ferryboats today is very small compared to their heyday during the early 1930s because of the construction of the San Francisco–Oakland Bay and Golden Gate Bridges. Back in the early thirties seventy-five thousand commuters daily rode the ferryboats to San Francisco's Ferry Building from a dozen long piers extending out into the bay from cities around the bay's perimeter. Not only did many ride the ferryboats, about ten thousand commuters took their cars with them daily.

If you would like to experience a ferry ride, wander down either to the Ferry Building at the foot of the Embarcadero or over to Fisherman's Wharf. From the Ferry Building ferryboats will take you to Oakland and Alameda; from Fisherman's Wharf you will get to Marin County. Taking your car with you can only be accommodated from the Ferry Building. The trip will cost more, but the experience of driving onto the ferryboat is unforgettable. The ferryboat is a 240-foot-long, steel-hulled vessel with one flat deck to accommodate cars and an enclosed lounge area for passengers.

Several minutes before the ferryboat docks, a line of cars begins to form. When the boat docks it empties its deck of cars before reloading for the return trip. One of the first things you will notice is that the ferryboat is double ended, meaning it loads and unloads from both ends. This odd arrangement allows the boat to sail back and forth without turning around, which would be a dangerous maneuver in a crowded harbor.

The ride from San Francisco to Oakland is just long enough to wander up to the restaurant and have a sandwich and something to drink while enjoying the view and the lazy roll of the boat. Ten minutes before docking the boat, the captain blows a warning whistle and orders all passengers to their cars so they can quickly clear the decks as soon as the boat docks. The ferryboat to Marin County, which departs from Fisherman's Wharf, is a quicker ride, but the boat does not accommodate cars.

The Ferry Building

On the eastern edge of the waterfront, beneath the San Francisco–Oakland Bay Bridge, stands the stately Ferry Building. One of the oldest among the

The Ferry Building, towering over a placid San Francisco Bay, was one of the few city structures to survive the 1906 earthquake.

Getting to Know the Diggers

While wandering the streets of San Francisco, do not be surprised if you suddenly encounter a theater group acting out a play in the middle of a street or a group of hippies giving away free clothes, flowers, and food. These carefree characters and their entertaining antics represent a social action group called the Diggers, whose credo in life is to reform San Francisco into the nation's first "free city."

The Diggers are famous throughout the San Francisco Bay Area for their spontaneous free street theater, free medical treatment, and free food giveaways that are part of their social agenda for creating a free city. Dressed in outrageously colorful and flamboyant costumes, their spontaneous dramatics stop traffic while they act out short skits to the delight of passersby. They also manage a free medical clinic called the Haight-Ashbury Free Medical Clinic. Their most famous activity revolves around distributing free food every day in Golden Gate Park and distributing surplus clothes, books, and trinkets at a series of stores where everything is free for the taking. Digger bread, a favorite among the homeless and the hippies, is easily recognizable by the distinctive shape of the one- and two-pound coffee cans in which it is baked.

Members of the social action group the Diggers distribute free food in Golden Gate park.

few survivors of the 1906 earthquake, this landmark is a friend known to all San Franciscans. With a sentinel clock tower standing 232 feet above the wharf, it was San Francisco's most recognizable landmark before the construction of the Golden Gate Bridge. As its name indicates, this facility was the main terminal for the dozens of ferryboats that plied the San Francisco Bay before the construction of the bridges.

Built in 1896 the Ferry Building was the city's tallest building. On each of the tower's four sides architects placed a large circular clock thirty feet in a diameter, which can easily be read by commuters from miles away.

A young architect named A. Page Brown drew up plans for the large steel-framed building. His original proposal for an 840-foot-long building plus tower was reduced to 660 feet. Although the Ferry Building is still port to ferryboats, it is nothing compared to its heyday thirty-five years ago. At its peak an average of fifty thousand commuters streamed through the building each day. San Francisco columnist Herb Caen once said that San Francisco without the Ferry Building's tall spire "would be like a birthday cake without a candle."[7]

Unconventional San Francisco

San Franciscans take pride in doing things differently from people in most cities. San Franciscans exhibit considerable tolerance toward people of every race, nationality, religion, sexual orientation, political conviction, and social status. The residents enjoy a reputation for allowing people to be completely free to be themselves, no matter how unconventional, nonconforming, or outrageous. Many San Franciscans are free thinkers who are not inclined to believe everything they read, see, or hear in the news, and they tend to question mass-marketed cultural values and heavily advertised consumer products.

Ever since the gold rush days San Francisco has celebrated and encouraged the thoughts and actions of eccentric personalities. The city's rich tradition includes such notable and quirky characters as Emperor Norton, the flamboyant and slightly wacky pauper who declared himself the emperor of the United States in 1859. Although penniless he was know by the city's elite, dined free in all of the city's restaurants, and when he died in 1880, thirty thousand attended his funeral. He was also the first to propose the oddball idea of building a bridge across the Golden Gate!

More recently and more seriously, during the 1920s, San Francisco became a haven for Marxists and Leninists supporting the Russian Revolution, which installed the world's first Communist government. In contradiction to America's official democratic policy, many San Franciscans marched the streets of San Francisco in support of what they saw as the beginning of a utopian world. In 1926 the British writer

The Beatnik-Hippie Connection

San Francisco is the recognized home of both the beat and hippie movements. Each espouses shared antiestablishment attitudes on a broad spectrum of political and social issues, even though each has a different foundation and perspective.

Although the beats and hippies span two different decades, have varied opinions on many cultural activities, and live in separate areas of San Francisco, their gravitation to the same city is not coincidental. According to Jerry Garcia, leader of the Grateful Dead, his early songs were inspired by beat writer Jack Kerouac's book, *On the Road,* as Garcia recently disclosed to writer Holly Georee-Warren, author of *The Rolling Stone Book of the Beats: The Beat Generation and Ameri-*

Beat writers Hal Chase, Jack Kerouac, Allen Ginsberg, and William Burroughs (from left) greatly influenced many of today's hippie artists.

can Culture. "I read it [*On the Road*] and fell in love with it, the adventure, the romance of it, everything. . . . I owe a lot of who I am and what I've been and what I've done to the beatniks from the fifties and to the poetry and art and music that I've come in contact with," said Garcia.

Gary Duncan, a member of the 1960s San Francisco rock group Quicksilver Messenger Service echoes Garcia, noting to George-Warren that: "The Haight-Ashbury scene is basically an outgrowth of the Beat Generation in North Beach."

To Allen Ginsberg, one of the few intellectuals bridging both movements, the hippie movement was a logical continuation of the beat movement. Quoted in George-Warren's book he said of 1960s folksinger Bob Dylan: "I think that, between Kerouac and myself, and Burroughs, there was quite an impact. Dylan told me that. I know Kerouac was a major inspiration for him as a poet."

Rudyard Kipling, who fell in love with San Francisco's unconventional behavior, proclaimed affectionately: "San Francisco is a mad city —inhabited for the most part by perfectly insane people."[8] This same sort of "mad" behavior continues to be tolerated today. California's Pulitzer Prize–winning writer John Steinbeck paid this tribute to San Francisco's willingness to embrace the unconventional, saying of it:

> Once I knew the City very well, spent my attic days there, while others were being a lost generation in Paris, I fledged [started] in San Francisco, climbed its hills, slept in its parks, worked on its docks, marched and shouted in its revolts. . . . It had been good to me in the days of my poverty and it did not resent my temporary solvency.[9]

John Steinbeck wrote fondly of his experiences in San Francisco as a struggling young writer.

Where else can anyone find so many idiosyncratic places and activities? At the City Lights Books bookstore, which advertises that it sells banned books; the annual foot race called the Bay to Breakers, known for the runners' bizarre costumes; and a nightclub where all the showgirls are men dressed as women. It comes as no surprise to San Franciscans that today the city is home to two of the most unconventional cultural movements in the city's history—the beats and the hippies.

Chapter 4

Five Classic Explorations

Much of San Francisco's distinctive charm will unfold as visitors head out into the city. A great way to start is to explore five of the classic locations that all first-time visitors ought to experience before returning home.

San Francisco Bay

The best way to experience the bay is by boat. Wander down to Fisherman's Wharf at the north end of the city and buy a ticket at Pier 39 to any one of the tour boats that cruises the bay. As the tour boat departs it heads first to the Golden Gate where it passes under the Golden Gate Bridge. As the boat makes its pass, everyone will have an opportunity to see close up the two massive concrete piers supporting the two tall towers soaring 746 feet above the waves. Each of these concrete piers extends below the waves to bedrock that contains about fifty thousand tons of concrete and steel reinforcing rods.

At the bridge you will get a feel for the turbulence of the water. The swirls and rivulets that appear benign at the surface mask deeper currents propelling one-sixth of the volume of the bay through the gate each day. At the rate of 2.3 million cubic feet per second, the surge is three-and-a-half times the volume of water that the Mississippi River disgorges into the Gulf of Mexico. Many weekend sailboaters caught in this narrow gap have found themselves swept miles out into the Pacific before being released from the current's grip.

After circling the bridge the boat will head east toward the most recognized island in the bay—Alcatraz. This island, which is just one-and-a-half miles off Fisherman's Wharf, was home to many of the nation's most desperate and hardened criminals until its closure in 1963. As your boat glides close by, the main cell block, lighthouse, walled exercise yard, and warden's house are clearly visible, as are the wooden guard towers, barbed wire fences, and officers' quarters. Alcatraz remains off limits to the public until some use for the island can be determined.

From Alcatraz the boat will circle north around Angel Island. This island, the largest in the bay, is one of the more enjoyable natural habitats set aside for weekend campers, hikers, and bicyclists. The few wooden structures seen as the boat passes by were part of an immigration station built here in 1905 to process immigrants entering the West Coast of the United States, primarily from Asia. For this reason Angel Island is often referred to as the "Ellis Island of the West Coast." As the boat heads back to Fisherman's Wharf, the bayside cities of Belvedere, Tiburon, and Sausalito can be seen on the right.

Fisherman's Wharf

The northeastern section of San Francisco's waterfront, known to everyone as Fisherman's Wharf, is the most visited

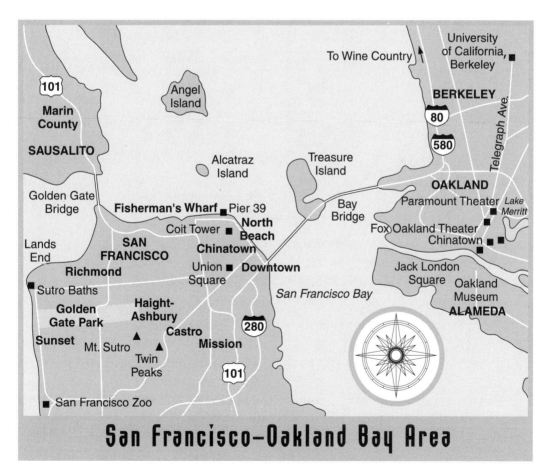

San Francisco–Oakland Bay Area

Visitors can board boats at Fisherman's Wharf that offer tours of San Francisco Bay.

tourist attraction in the city. Every day this area surges with gawking tourists jostling each other. The wharf has two personalities. It is part a cheesy whirl of souvenir shops selling typically tourist items such as fake Alcatraz prisoner uniforms, miniature soap carvings of cable cars, and endless paintings of the Golden Gate Bridge. The wharf is also part restaurant row, featuring a dozen or so seafood eateries all offering fresh catch and dramatic views of the bay. This may be the one place that native San Franciscans refuse to frequent. The only natives you are likely to find here are the Dungeness crabs boiling in the huge cauldrons that line the sidewalks in front of restaurants.

The wharf's name derives from before World War II when the only activity along the wharf was the unloading of the local fishing fleet that docked here. Winched out of the holds of the boats each evening were tons of crab, yellowtail, tuna, flounder, ling cod, and other Pacific species. Then, in the late 1940s, a few fishermen hit on the idea of opening small family restaurants and selling their catch to hungry tourists. Within a few years the wharf took off as a popular place to soak up the local waterfront culture.

Do not let the tackiness of the place deter you—there are interesting things to do and see. Start with what is called a "walk-away" lunch of fresh crab that will be pulled from the huge steaming cauldrons, cracked right in front of you, and served in a paper dish with a piece of the city's equally famous sourdough bread. With crab in hand, take a tour of a wooden schooner built in the 1880s, the *Balcultha*. This ship is three hundred feet long and has three masts. The *Balcultha* is a square-rigger, which describes the con-

figuration of the sails when they are unfurled. Although no longer in service, this was the sort of ship that littered the wharf area in San Francisco by the hundreds at the turn of the century.

A cook removes two Dungeness crabs from a cauldron in front of his Fisherman's Wharf restaurant.

Bay to Breakers Run

Each May thousands of San Franciscans participate in a seven-and-a-half-mile race called the Bay to Breakers run. It takes its name from the start point at the bay near the Embarcadero and winds its way west through Golden Gate Park to the breakers of the Pacific Ocean.

This foot race is one of those San Francisco traditions that is truly a one-of-a-kind, wacky event. Although the Bay to Breakers run is a legitimate race with prize money awarded to the winners, the true spirit of the race—which sets it apart from all other races—is its carnival atmosphere of fun and laughter for the majority of the partici-

Runners crowd a San Francisco street during the city's annual Bay to Breakers run.

pants. Typical Bay to Breakers traditions include runners wearing an assortment of circus, animal, and plant costumes; groups of participants running in choreographed patterns; runners with their pet dogs; bands playing along the race route; and a variety of merry pranksters simply enjoying the day with no intentions of finishing the race.

The Bay to Breakers race began in 1912, six years after the great earthquake, as a way to boost the city's battered spirits. A showplace for the city's irrepressible color and its affection for bizarre traditions, Bay to Breakers is today one of the most beloved civic festivals. Over the years the race has mushroomed in size, drawing fifty thousand participants in 1966 and more than two hundred thousand spectators.

Once on board visitors are free to wander the ship. Of greatest interest to most is a tour of the cargo hold below the top deck. This cavernous storage area was used for many transatlantic voyages transporting up to 2,650 tons of coal from England, wheat from California, salmon from Alaska, Scotch whiskey from Glasgow, and iron from Liverpool. Also of interest are the ship's quarters for the twenty-six-man crew. The captain's stateroom is the most luxurious of all the quarters, with private bathroom, mahogany-paneled work space for plotting the ship's course, and an elegant bedroom with brass lamps. This luxury was due in part to his rank and in part because he was permitted to have his wife accompany him.

Three blocks west down North Point Street, past more curio shops and restaurants, is Ghirardelli Square, the nicest shopping area on the wharf. Named after the chocolate company, this site was at one time the company's chocolate manufacturing plant. In 1964 it was converted into dozens of chic shops selling clothes, fine art, books and posters, cappuccino and espresso, candles, and—of course—Ghirardelli chocolates that are now produced elsewhere in the city.

Chinatown

At the southeast corner of Ghirardelli Square is a cable car turnaround where you can catch the Powell-Hyde (PH) cable car that will take you to the third recommended stop—Chinatown. Ride the cable car until the gripman or brakeman hollers out, "Chinatown." Hop off and you will instantaneously be immersed in a foreign and mystical culture. This unique neighborhood in San Francisco derives its name from the Chinese who initially came here to mine for gold in the late 1840s. In 1863, however, when few had made any money, thousands went to work building the transcontinental railroad. About ten thousand Chinese worked for the Central Pacific Railroad and were largely responsible for building the western leg from Sacramento up over the rugged Sierra Nevada mountain range to Promontory Point, Utah. During and after this twenty-year period, Chinatown flourished. Many Chinese settled here to find work and raise their families.

Chinatown today is as much a sightseeing requirement as Fisherman's Wharf and the bay. Even locals continue to come here to breathe in a unique and exotic cultural experience. Roughly eight blocks long by four blocks wide, this densely packed neighborhood of thirty thousand—most of whom speak Cantonese as their primary language—remains the largest Chinese neighborhood outside of Asia.

Chinatown's crowded streets are choked with Chinese-speaking residents dressed in traditional clothes. The streets are always crowded with residents who spend most of their days on the streets and with the many small family-owned markets that sell a variety of traditional foods. Dead, plucked chickens hang by their necks; live fish swim in tanks of water; small wooden baskets are filled with live baby quail. Set on the sidewalks in front of shops are barrels filled with dried animal organs that include bear and tiger gallbladders and kidneys. Other baskets hold dried shark fins for shark-fin soup. Inside the shops garlands of exotic herbs hang from the walls, and the smell of burning incense permeates the rooms.

Non-Chinese visitors may feel uneasy wandering down alleys crowded with apartments; hidden temples; curio shops; traditional red, orange, and green paper lanterns; and busy restaurants. Even the street signs are in Chinese as well as English. Red, gold, and green lampposts, installed in 1925, are made of cast iron with carvings of bamboo and are surrounded by carvings of a pair of coiled dragons. In the narrow streets and alleys children still play with firecrackers that are meant to chase off bad luck when they explode. Although firecrackers are illegal in San Francisco, these brief minor explosions are recognized as an important component of Chinese culture and no one seems to complain.

Stroll all the way to the south end of Grant Avenue and walk through the elaborately decorated Chinatown Gate that symbolically separates Chinatown from one of San Francisco's most expensive and most elegant shopping areas around Union Square. This gate is in the traditional Chinese form with its broad, curving, colorfully painted, vertical and horizontal wooden beams.

Haight-Ashbury

From Chinatown take the bus or drive out to the Golden Gate Park Panhandle to the intersection of Haight and Ashbury. The Haight-Ashbury neighborhood along the eastern edge of Golden Gate Park has become a magnet for the youthful hippie culture that began a couple of years ago. As word of the free-spirited youth culture spread, thousands hitchhiked here from all over the United States to live communally on the streets and in shared apartments. Since last year the streets have been awash with those who are openly experimenting with the latest psychedelic drugs, begging on the streets for money, sharing everything they own, and generally denouncing the conservative "straight world" of their parents.

The Haight, as this area is more commonly called, attracted little attention until a handful of beat writers settled here in the early 1960s. Allen Ginsberg and a few

Alcatraz

The Alcatraz Island that tour boats circle is no longer a federal penitentiary. Once the infamous home to prisoners known as the Birdman of Alcatraz, Scarface Capone, and Machine Gun Kelly, Alcatraz ceased functioning as a federal penitentiary in 1963 because of excessive maintenance costs. What will become of the island has not yet been decided, but the legends of some of its most infamous inmates continue to attract public attention.

Long before Alcatraz was a federal penitentiary, it served as a military fort and prison. Although the population was never very large, the military spent enormous sums of money to level part of the island, construct an enormous cell block to house prisoners, build a lighthouse, and set up quarters for guards. The military, however, was in the business of defending America from foreign enemies, not imprisoning its own soldiers.

In 1932, J. Edgar Hoover, the director of the FBI, or-

dered the modernization of Alcatraz for a federal maximum security prison. A more secure cell block was constructed, along with machine-gun towers and a variety of escape-proof security features. When the prison opened it immediately earned the name The Rock, a reference to its rocky profile.

The Alcatraz prison building sits perched atop a rocky island in San Francisco Bay.

other writers moved here and the area acquired a new reputation as an intellectual and cultural center. But it really has not been more than three or four years since that it became an internationally celebrated neighborhood with the arrival of the hippies. Today music greats such as the Grateful Dead, Janis Joplin, Eric Clapton,

Country Joe and the Fish, and a handful of other musicians and their bands live here.

As you wander the streets, you will immediately notice that the hippies cultivate an offbeat look. Long hair pulled back in ponytails is favored by most men, and beards are more common here than

North Beach, Chinatown, and Telegraph Hill

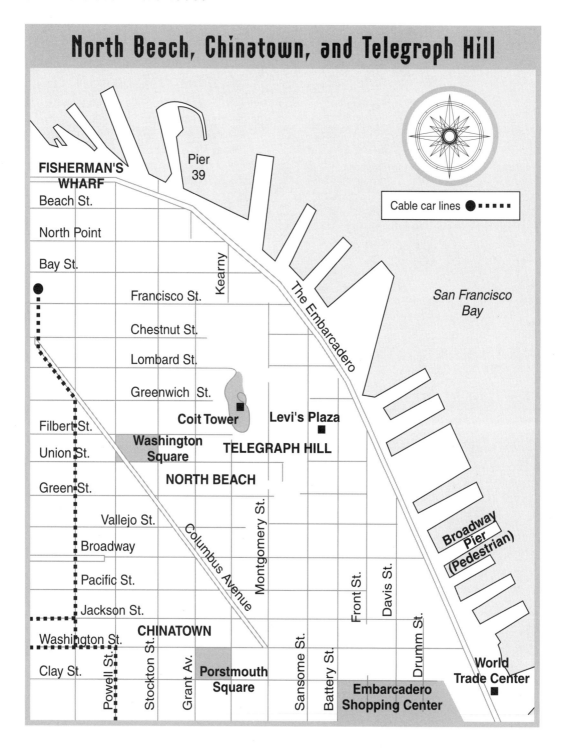

FISHERMAN'S WHARF

Pier 39

Beach St.

North Point

Bay St.

Francisco St.

Kearny

The Embarcadero

San Francisco Bay

Cable car lines ●▪▪▪▪▪

Chestnut St.

Lombard St.

Greenwich St.

Coit Tower

Levi's Plaza

Filbert St.

Washington Square

TELEGRAPH HILL

Union St.

NORTH BEACH

Green St.

Vallejo St.

Montgomery St.

Columbus Avenue

Broadway Pier (Pedestrian)

Broadway

Pacific St.

Jackson St.

Front St.

Davis St.

Drumm St.

Washington St.

CHINATOWN

World Trade Center

Clay St.

Powell St.

Stockton St.

Grant Av.

Porstmouth Square

Sansome St.

Battery St.

Embarcadero Shopping Center

Jerry Garcia, founder of the Grateful Dead, stands beneath the street sign at Haight and Ashbury.

anywhere else. Flamboyantly dressed in multicolored tie-dyed shirts and skirts, leather sandals, strings of beads, and old-fashioned clothes like their grandparents once wore, hippies can be seen strolling down the streets to blaring rock music, handing out flowers picked in Golden Gate Park, flashing the peace sign to each other, and openly smoking marijuana.

The fundamental nature of the Haight experience is sharing. Although most hippies living here do not have much, as a general rule whatever they have they share with each other. Apartments, more commonly called crash pads, are places where people may stay for a night or two and then move on. Most are overcrowded because they are shared by many low-income renters in order to pay the rent. Food is also shared by those who have it, and many local restaurants and small grocery stores place unused food on trays and set it out on their back porches at night so the scavengers, as they are called, can come by and pick it up for their free meals. Money is also shared. San Francisco's

Hip Vocabulary

The hippie culture has generated a handful of new terms used to describe some of the nuances of their culture, thinking, and activities. The following is a short list of the more commonly used terms:

Boss: Something is the best or very good.

Cool: OK, acceptable, interesting, statement of understanding or agreement.

Far out: A thing or experience that is surprisingly good or pleasurable.

Freak: A person acting out of control because of drugs or bizarre behavior.

Groovy: Something particularly interesting, or a feeling that all is well.

Heavy: Something that is hard to understand or deeply philosophical.

Hip: An understanding of what is acceptable and fashionable.

Hipster: A person obsessed with what is hip.

Mellow: Relaxed, calm, and content.

Munchies: Craving for snack food after smoking marijuana.

Right on: A term meaning "I agree," or an expression that something is correct.

Stoned: The mental state of experiencing the effects of a drug.

Trip: A drug session.

Tripping: Experiencing the effects of drug.

Wasted: Overdosed on a drug but not in danger.

Bishop Pike said of the hippies' Christian value of sharing that: "There is something about these people, a gentleness, a quietness, and interest—something good."[10] If you come here and do not adopt the stereotyped hippie look, expect to be greeted by panhandlers who will approach you offering a flower in their outstretched hands asking for money or a meal.

The city is bracing for even more hippies this summer for what many are already calling the Summer of Love. All of the major rock bands have agreed to play free concerts in nearby Golden Gate Park, while poets and left-wing politico-pranksters like Jerry Rubin and Abbie Hoffman are promising to organize antiwar marches throughout the city and in the East Bay area.

The Cliff House

From the Haight due west to the ocean is San Francisco's venerable Cliff House. This hotel-restaurant is a pleasant throwback to the turn of the century. Extending precariously over the surf at Seal Rock, the Cliff House has catered to upscale patrons since its inception in 1896. Expect to pay a princely sum to spend the night, since this is a favorite hotel for presidents, prima donnas, and the social elite from around the world. The most expensive rooms are those that extend out over the surf, and the most expensive meals are those specifically ordered by wealthy patrons. One of the nice features of the

Hippies relax in their Haight-Ashbury home. Hippies in this district typically share everything, including living spaces.

Cliff House is its availability for tours, even if you are only coming for lunch.

There are several attractions for people to visit after making this trip out to the coast. Except in winter, when the fog is thick and cold, people can also walk among the statues in the elaborate gardens above the Cliff House, on the grounds of Sutro Heights. There is also a sky tram that carries passengers along the water's edge between the Cliff House and Point Lobos. Just down the hill from the Cliff House is a large amusement park called Playland, and a two-minute walk directly north of the Cliff House are the famous and elaborate Sutro Baths. They have been renovated many times and continue to be enjoyed by bathers and swimmers.

One of the more fun activities is to pay a visit to the Camera Obscura. For one dollar you can enter the small, cir-

The Cliff House (shown here with Seal Rock in the background) is one of the city's most upscale and expensive hotel-restaurants. The Camera Obscura is just to the left of the Cliff House.

The owner of Cliff House looks at an image of Seal Rock projected inside the small, circular theater known as the Camera Obscura.

cular theater where projected on the walls is a 360-degree image of everything outside. Through a series of periscopes and mirrors that capture all movement outside, you will see projected on the walls the crashing surf, people walking by, and the seagulls that swoop down looking for a bite to eat.

Four different variations of the Cliff House have stood on these rocky cliffs at the northwest corner of San Francisco.

Two earlier versions were rather modestly small, especially when compared with the elaborate eight-story Victorian building that stood on the spot from 1896 to 1907 as the third Cliff House. And when that ornate version of the building burned down, the fourth version built, the one you see today, was designed more like the first two: simple, and made to blend in with the ocean and cliffs surrounding it.

Chapter 5

Four Unforgettable Walks

Calmer than the Haight, Fisherman's Wharf, and Chinatown, yet just as fascinating as the Cliff House are four recommended walks to interesting parts of San Francisco missed by many tourists.

The Golden Gate Bridge

The Golden Gate Bridge is consistently the city's most often photographed, most visited, most beloved, and most sought-out site for Hollywood film producers in the city. Since its completion thirty years ago, in 1937, this beautiful red-orange bridge has become the city's defining symbol. Plan to take a walk across the Golden Gate's famed span; it is one of life's memorable experiences. Two hundred and fifty feet above the surging waters of the deep Pacific Ocean, a combination of vertigo, high winds, and the sway of the roadway will have

first-timers gripping the guard rail with white knuckles.

The south approach to the bridge, which is part of Highway 101, is easy to find by car or tour bus. Once there walk or bicycle across the east side to slowly savor the experience. There is no bad time to cross the bridge as long as you are not in a car. The views are spectacular by day or night, and if it feels like the bridge is moving on a windy day, it is; the Golden Gate was engineered to sway twenty-seven feet from side to side so it will not snap in powerful, gale-force winds. Only twice have engineers closed the bridge because of excessive sway.

As walkers set out toward the Marin County side, the intended slight upward arc at the center of the bridge will be evident. Stop at either of the towers and marvel at its height and strength. Each of the nubs protruding on the surface is a rivet, the steel pins that hold the steel plates together, and each tower has six hundred thousand of them. Now crane your head straight up. The sensation of the clouds whipping by will instinctively cause even the most spirited hiker to reach back to catch his or her balance.

Midway across the bridge stop for a moment and take in the view of San Francisco off to the right, then the slightly older San Francisco–Oakland Bay Bridge. Shifting your view to the left is Alcatraz Island dead ahead one mile, and Angel Island next to it.

A walk across the Golden Gate Bridge is a must for all visitors to San Francisco.

Berkeley is back on the East Bay, and off to the left the third and most recent of the great bridges on the bay, the Richmond–San Rafael Bridge. Finally, off to the extreme left, the quaint Marin County seaside towns of Bel- vedere, Tiburon, and Sausalito can be seen.

The Golden Gate Bridge is a beauty recently named one of the Seven Won- ders of the Modern World by the Amer- ican Society of Civil Engineers. Few believed that head engineer, Joseph Strauss, could build the longest suspen- sion bridge of its time. Today, in addi- tion to hundreds who make the gusty walk each day, it is the daily commute for tens of thousands of workers be- tween Marin County and downtown San Francisco.

What Holds Up the Golden Gate Bridge?

Most pedestrians crossing the Golden Gate Bridge mistakenly believe that the roadway on which they are walking and over which commuters drive is se- cured by the bridge's twin 746-foot-high towers. Although the massive steel towers play a role in supporting the roadway, they are not what keeps it from collapsing into the bay.

Engineers who built this mile-long sus- pension bridge explain that the weight of the roadway is secured by four massive concrete anchors—two buried deep within the earth at each end of the bridge. Each of the four anchors is nearly one hundred thousand cubic feet, weighs about 64,000 tons, and is capable of re- sisting 32,500 tons of pull without budging so much as a millimeter. Attached to each anchor is one end of each of the two main cables that loop up and over the two tow- ers. The towers simply support the cables and give them their familiar graceful arc. Attached to each main cable are 125 sus- pender cables spaced fifty feet apart that attach to the roadway. Although the tow- ers, main cables, and suspender cables help support the roadway, the four an- chors support the entire structure.

Angel Island

Often referred to as the jewel of the San Francisco Bay, Angel Island is the largest and most bucolic island in the bay. For these reasons it is a great place to spend an unforgettable day. This gem of the California state park system offers panoramic vistas of the entire bay. Sightseers will enjoy picture-postcard views of the San Francisco skyline, the hills of Marin County, Alcatraz, and Mount Tamalpis seventeen miles away. A clear day on the island is referred to as a five-bridge day because from the is- land's highest point, Mount Livermore, hikers can view the Golden Gate, San Francisco–Oakland Bay, Richmond– San Rafael, San Mateo, and the Dum- barton Bridges. Mount Livermore is 781 feet high and was named after Caroline Livermore, a Marin County conserva- tionist who led the campaign to create Angel Island State Park.

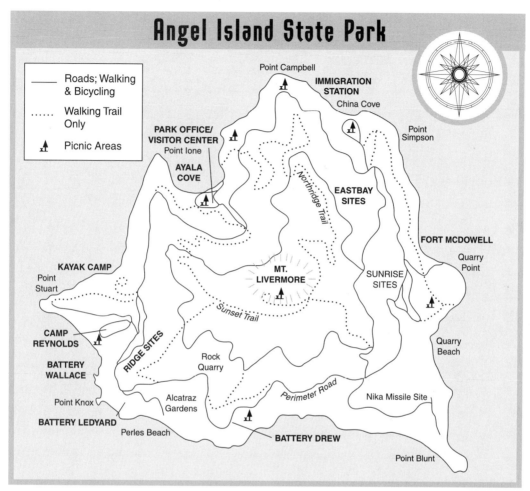

Angel Island State Park

Roads; Walking & Bicycling

...... Walking Trail Only

⚓ Picnic Areas

Point Campbell

IMMIGRATION STATION

China Cove

PARK OFFICE/ VISITOR CENTER
Point Ione

Point Simpson

AYALA COVE

Northridge Trail

EASTBAY SITES

FORT MCDOWELL

Quarry Point

KAYAK CAMP

Point Stuart

MT. LIVERMORE

SUNRISE SITES

Sunset Trail

CAMP REYNOLDS

RIDGE SITES

Rock Quarry

Quarry Beach

BATTERY WALLACE

Point Knox

Alcatraz Gardens

Perimeter Road

Nika Missile Site

BATTERY LEDYARD

Perles Beach

BATTERY DREW

Point Blunt

To get to Angel Island take the ferry from either San Francisco or Tiburon. One of the best ways to explore this historic 740-acre island is by walking the five-mile perimeter trail. Starting at Ayala Cove, where most of the ferries land, and walking counterclockwise around the island, you will pass World War II artillery batteries, modern Cold War Nike missile sites that remain operational, a Civil War military fort, and the old Immigration Station.

Perhaps of greatest historical interest is the Immigration Station built in 1910. This station was designed to handle the arrival of European immigrants when the Panama Canal opened. The station wound up handling mostly Chinese immigrants. The station closed in 1940 after nearly two hundred thousand Chinese had been processed. The adjacent museum provides a photographic historical record of Chinese immigration to the United States. Ranger-led tours

The Immigrant Station (immigrant dormitory is pictured) is just one of the attractions for visitors to Angel Island.

are offered on summer weekends, and it is important to bear in mind that visitation hours are from 8:00 A.M. to sunset.

Not only is the island a delight for history buffs, nature lovers can enjoy miles of hiking and biking trails with breathtaking views around every bend. Bicycles are available for rent, as are kayaks that can be paddled around the island to take advantage of the coastline, which from the water offers a unique way to enjoy the island's scenic beauty. After an active day of exploring,

why not relax with a cappuccino or complete lunch at the Cove Café prior to your departure?

North Beach

North Beach, as the name indicates, occupies the north end of the city; specifically, the northeast shoulder of the city edged by bay. Its most notable landmark, Telegraph Hill, is situated at its most northeastern point. Today this neighborhood of several dozen blocks has many personalities, each of which attracts residents and travelers for different reasons.

For some residents North Beach is San Francisco's "Little Italy," with street names reflecting its heritage; Columbus Avenue, for example, is the main artery slicing through the district. The scent of olive oil used for cooking is carried through the district from restaurants with unmistakable Italian names such as the Fior d'Italia, Buon Gusto, and Café Roma serving authentic Italian cuisine. Found here too are dozens of old-world delicatessens with traditional red-and-white-checked tablecloths where soups and an

assortment of sandwiches made from cheeses and spiced meats are served. At the corner of Valparaiso and Taylor Streets locals proudly point out the house where Joe DiMaggio was born, the legendary baseball slugger with the New York Yankees who was recently elected to the Baseball Hall of Fame. San Francisco's current mayor, Joseph Alioto, the son of an Italian immigrant, also grew up on the streets and in the parks of North Beach.

This neighborhood is home to a group of writers and poets known to the literary world as the beats. Like members of other artistic movements, the beat writers are a

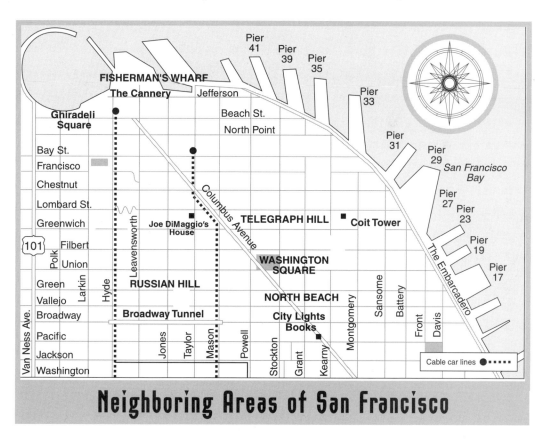

Neighboring Areas of San Francisco

Neal Cassady (center left), Allen Ginsberg (center), Lawrence Ferlinghetti (far right), and other beat writers meet outside City Lights in 1956.

small group of close friends who embrace an unconventional bohemian lifestyle contrary to mainstream America. Denouncing materialism, capitalism, conservative government policies, and most forms of social conformity, the beats as a group espouse living simple, spiritual lives committed to encouraging individuality and social concern for the poor and oppressed.

Many beats affect the bohemian avant-garde look by wearing old, dark-colored clothes too tattered for most San Franciscans. Tourists wandering the streets

of North Beach expect to see the beatniks, as they are called. Bruce Conner, a North Beach artist and resident, finds it amusing that they are of interest to tourists. He commented:

People would call me a beatnik just because of the way I dressed. I wore the least expensive clothes that would allow me to paint and would last a long time: tennis shoes, jeans, sweatshirts. It was easy to be a weekend beatnik. All you had to do was dress like that. On the weekends, there were hundreds of tourists coming through to look at the beatniks. They would talk about the beatniks as if they were looking at animals in the zoo.[11]

Still seen today occasionally wandering the streets of North Beach are the core of the West Coast beat writers: Jack Kerouac, Allen Ginsberg, Neal Cassady, Gregory Corso, Gary Snyder, Lawrence Ferlinghetti, Michael Mc-Clure, and Philip Whalen.

One of the major reasons this area is a literary haven is City Lights Books bookstore on the corner of Columbus Avenue and Broadway. This is an enduring

City Lights Books Bookstore

Sitting at the intersection of Columbus Avenue and Broadway, this bookstore is the most recognized literary icon in the city. Writer Bill Urlaub provided this insightful description: "City Lights Books is unconventional, iconoclastic, anarchistic, and about as anti-establishment as an establishment can get. As America's first and only 'Literary Landmark,' City Lights is proud of its Beatnik origins and its anti-authoritarian attitude."[1]

San Francisco beat poet Lawrence Ferlinghetti, owner of City Lights, brought fame to the bookstore in 1957 when he published Allen Ginsberg's book of poems, *Howl*, which the courts banned as being obscene. Ferlinghetti was arrested but successfully fought the case in court, earning him and his bookstore the reputation as a publishing house that would publish any work with literary merit. In mock defiance of the courts following his vindication, Ferlinghetti placed a sign in the front window of his bookstore that read: "WE SELL BANNED BOOKS." According to writer Robert Hass, poet Gary Snyder commented some years later: "By this time [1966], City Lights was obviously playing a very vibrant role in the whole counterculture evolution."[2]

Inside the bookstore, browsers are not likely to find mainstream books and magazines. Instead City Lights stocks the works of beat writers, several shelves of French and Italian poets, Russian writers who openly express their contempt for their government, the classics of established intellectuals, and foreign-language magazines from around the world. One of the bookstore's favorite features enjoyed by San Franciscans is the availability of sofas and benches for comfortable reading. In the same article, "City Lights and the Counterculture," artist Bruce Conner commented: "I moved here from Kansas in '57. City Lights was like a clubhouse. Lawrence made it convenient for you to just sit there for hours and read the books, like a library. City Lights had some of the most sophisticated graffiti in the bathroom commenting about Greek classics, or Shakespeare."[3]

1. "America's Only Literary Landmark," *Guardsman Online*, 2001. www.theguardsman.com.
2. "City Lights and The Counterculture," *SFgate.com*, September 2002. www.sfgate.com.
3. "The Fall of San Francisco; Some Personal Observations," *S.F. Heart*, 2002. www.sfheart.com.

icon of North Beach and a valuable resource for new voices in literature. Founded by Lawrence Ferlinghetti in 1953, City Lights Books is now the center of gravity for the beat movement. Still owned by Ferlinghetti, City Lights continues to support freethinking writers and poets who rarely become mainstream authors. Bibliophiles should take the opportunity to stop in and explore the shelves of books, many of which will not be found elsewhere.

Just a few blocks down the street, at Columbus and Union Streets, is Washington Square, one of San Francisco's many neighborhood parks. This one square block of trees, lawns, playgrounds, and park benches is a perfect spot to rest with a cold drink and Italian sausage sandwich before moving on. The statue on the corner is not of an Italian but rather a Philadelphian; it is that of Benjamin Franklin and it was donated to the city in 1879 by a San Franciscan who made his fortune during the gold rush.

The Marina

If there are still a few hours left in the afternoon, not far from North Beach is the fourth recommended walk, the Marina. Take Columbus all the way to the bay, turn left, and another mile walk will take you to the Marina, just east of the Golden Gate Bridge, down at water's edge.

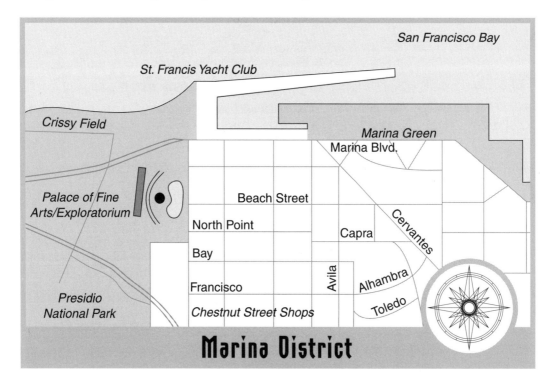

Marina District

A hippie purchases a small-press book of poetry at City Lights.

A walk along the Marina in the afternoon before the fog rolls in will have something for everyone. The Marina combines expensive, elegant homes; the exclusive St. Francis Yacht Club; a long, rectangular park called Crissy Field; the Palace of Fine Arts; and the Exploratorium. Within a few blocks walkers will experience all of these pleasures unique to San Francisco.

The Marina is the result of landfill over the past one hundred years needed to expand the city to accommodate population growth. During the gold-rush years, this valuable land was part of the San Francisco wharf area where sail-ing ships loaded and unloaded their cargo. Today, whenever the foundation for a new home or business is dug, archaeologists swarm over the site examining old ship masts, anchor chains, and rudders with Chinese characters identifying the ship's home port.

In 1915 the Palace of Fine Arts was built to celebrate the opening of the Panama Canal. As the leading port on the West Coast, San Francisco was the principal beneficiary of the canal. The exhibition was considered to be a World's Fair showcasing San Francisco and it involved the construction of the stately and beautiful Palace of Fine Arts. This complex

The Exploratorium

One of the great new "fun zones" recently added to San Francisco's collection of unusual cultural centers is the Exploratorium housed in the Palace of Fine Arts at the Marina. This is more than another place to have fun; it is a laboratory dedicated to the enjoyable exploration of science.

Visitors enter and immediately find themselves walking through a light show of multicolored laser beams (beams of light bouncing off reflectors) and an exhibit reproducing the famous experiment that first accurately measured the speed of light. From here you can choose to visit any of several rooms, each of which focuses on one of a variety of scientific principles of physics, chemistry, astronomy, geology, seismology, meteorology, and other scientific fields.

Sometimes you will crawl, climb, or slide your way through the best science museum in the world. With more than 650 hands-on exhibits, everyone discovers the wonders of science and technology and have a great time doing it. Simulation allows you to build your own solar system, explore Antarctica, or take a peek through the world's largest two-hundred-inch telescope on Palomar Mountain in California.

One of the strengths of the Exploratorium is its staff's ability to present demonstrations and experiments coinciding with rare natural events. During a solar eclipse, for example, the staff will set up solar-system demonstrations that explain the principles involved in the eclipse and the mathematics that astronomers use to accurately predict eclipses for millions of years into the future.

Children participate in a hands-on science lesson at the Exploratorium.

Built in 1915, the Palace of Fine Arts is a complex of domes and columns built in the Greco-Roman style.

encircles a beautiful lake, and the many domes and columns create the effect of walking in ancient Rome. The lake is home to white swans that lazily move about the water as tourists quietly enjoy floral-decorated walks through forty-foot-high colonnades.

Housed within the walls of the Palace of Fine Arts is the Exploratorium. This new science exhibition houses a collection of more than 650 displays. The unique museum was founded last year by noted physicist and educator Dr. Frank Oppenheimer who devoted his efforts to it. Inside students will find experiments demonstrating many of the most important scientific principles. This hall of science is known for its quality of instruction and for the fun that visiting students enjoy while learning about science.

Across the street from the Exploratorium is Crissy Field at the bay's edge. This long, one-hundred-acre, rectangular expanse of green lawn was a landing field for single-propeller airplanes in the 1920s. Today it is San Francisco's favorite playland for kite flyers, Frisbee throwers, picnickers, joggers, sunbathers, and dog owners.

Just to the west of the Marina is the St. Francis Yacht Club. Although the club is private, indulge your temptation to walk along the docks and take in the beauty of some of San Francisco's most elegant yachts. Whether you prefer powerboats to the elegance of sailing sloops silently cutting through the water, each type of craft is a work of art.

Chapter 6

Four Hills of Distinction

Not far from the Marina is another favorite historic walking tour. This one consists of hills. San Francisco encompasses dozens of hilltop neighborhoods sculpted on graceful slopes rising from the bay. Each hill is valued for its unique, natural treasures, and each has its own special panoramic view of colorful sailboats splashed across the swells of the bay, of tree-lined streets zigzagging their way down to the water's edge, and myriad of eclectic cultural offerings. Even the fog, commonly found in all coastal communities, is enjoyed by locals as it poetically shrouds the hills in a mantle of white.

Many of the sidewalks in these neighborhoods are virtually staircases. It is not unusual to start walking only to find yourself hiking up staircases because of the extreme steepness of the hill. Free-standing staircases made of both wood and concrete rise above the

ground on wood and stone pilings as they switchback across the hilly terrain. Before riding to the top of any of the four recommended hills in your car or bus, consider finding one of the many walkways and footpaths that will make the trip to the top all the more memorable.

Telegraph Hill

In a city famous for its hills, Telegraph Hill is the highest, at 284 feet above its rock base in the North Beach neighborhood. To get here drive or take a bus to the base of the hill and then enjoy one of the city's most serene walks to the top. As you approach the base on Lombard, look for the concrete staircase on the north side and head up through the pine and spruce trees. As you work your way to the top, take a few moments to stop and look at the trendy apartments that command views of the city and bay.

The name Telegraph Hill was chosen during the early days of the gold rush when San Francisco was quickly becoming the busiest port on the West Coast. With hundreds of great, billowy sailed schooners from around the world entering and departing the bay, a lookout was posted on top of the hill to telegraph the arrival of ships to those below. A tall pole with movable arms was erected on the crest of the hill. Adjusting the arms and raising a country's flag alerted officials throughout the city to the arrival and nationality of each ship.

This inventive mechanical signaling system did not last long. In 1853, the pole with movable arms was made obsolete by the electric telegraph. Although Telegraph Hill continued to play a critical role in the dissemination of shipping news, its importance gradually declined and it was abandoned as a telegraph station, except when the 1906 earthquake set the city on fire and the fire chief sent signal men up the hill to help spot the fires.

Hikers are treated to a spectacular view when they reach the summit. The steep grades of the hill provide tremendous views of downtown San Francisco; all three of the bay's bridges; Angel, Alcatraz, and Yerba Buena Islands; Marin County; and the East Bay. After picking out all of the famous sites, enter and climb to the top of Coit Tower that dominates the summit.

The view from the top of Telegraph Hill's Coit Tower is one of the most spectacular in the city. Alcatraz Island is in the background.

In 1931 the will of Lillie Hitchcock Coit, an eccentric San Franciscan and honorary member of the San Francisco Fire Department, specified that her $118,731 inheritance was to be spent on an "artistic monument to the memory of the original Volunteer Fire Department."[12] To honor her request, two years later the 180-foot tower that stands here was formally dedicated to the city's volunteer firefighters who fought so valiantly to control the fires of the 1906 earthquake. Most San Franciscans believe the tower has the appearance of a fire-hose nozzle. While there are interesting murals inside painted by Diego Rivera, the real attraction is the view from the top.

When you depart Telegraph Hill and are on your way down, take the Filbert Street steps down the east side to Montgomery Street and enjoy views of private cottages and exotic gardens along the way. As you descend you may be entertained by a flock of wild parrots that have made these trees their home.

Nob Hill

Nob Hill is San Francisco's swankiest hill. Looming 376 feet above the city it sits between Chinatown, North Beach, and the Financial District. Take the Powell Street cable car to get here because it is one of the great cable car rides in the city. As the cable car approaches the steep hill you will hear a metallic ratcheting sound as the gripman pulls back on the lever that grips the cable below the street, pulling the car sharply up the hill.

Nob Hill is so steep that in the early years of the city, horse-drawn carriages could not climb it. During this time, it was only sparsely inhabited by people willing to walk up the steep incline. It was not until the advent of cable cars that Nob Hill became a glitzy, fashionable address for those who had made fortunes in mining, railroads, and business. The most famous who built mansions up here to take in the views of the bay and downtown district were the Big Four: Mark Hopkins, Charles Crocker, Collis Huntington, and Leland Stanford, all of whom built mansions here from the profits they made building the transcontinental railroad. However, the earthquake of 1906 collapsed their stately homes.

While you wind around the top of the hill, four dominant structures will capture your attention: two landmark hotels, the Mark Hopkins and the Fairmont; Grace Cathedral on the west end; and the Flood mansion that stands just east of the beautiful park in the center of the hill. The enormous Flood mansion was built by James C. Flood, who made his fortune mining silver in Nevada. The mansion is built of Connecticut brownstone and surrounded by the most expensive bronze fence in the city. Today the mansion is the property of the Pacific Union Club, an exclusive private social club known sarcastically as the P-U to nonmembers. Although the grand staircase to the front porch is tempting, do not waste your time approaching the entry because the doorman will sternly turn away all non-members.

Cut across beautiful Huntington Park that is perpetually covered in flowers and has as its centerpiece the Fountain of the Turtles. Off to your left is Grace Cathedral, a gothic cathedral worth a visit primarily because of its enormous bronze entry doors. The doors are copies of doors that grace the Baptistery of San Giovanni in Florence, Italy. The sculpted doors stand sixteen feet high and weigh thirty-four thousand pounds. Each of the twin doors has five sculpted panels depicting scenes from the Old Testament, such as the creation of Adam, the sacrifice of Abel, the drunkenness of Noah, and Moses receiving the Ten Commandments. If time permits, wander inside the cavernous cathedral and you might be treated to an organ recital on the city's finest pipe organ.

Visitors to upscale Nob Hill (pictured) should not miss Huntington Park, Flood Mansion, and the area's many extravagant mansions and hotels.

Russian Hill

Between Nob Hill and Fisherman's Wharf is elegant and picturesque Russian Hill. The hill and the neighborhood surrounding it got its name when 1850s gold miners stumbled across seven gravestones inscribed in the Russian language at the top of the hill. No one knows for certain who the dead men were but the presence of Russian fur traders along the California coast before the gold rush suggests they might have been trappers. Today the gravestones are gone and the location of the graves forgotten.

The views from the top of Russian Hill are amazing, even more so than from Nob Hill. From up here looking north, each north-south street cuts a visual swath to the bay, revealing in long, narrow vistas Alcatraz Island, Fisherman's Wharf, Angel Island, the Marina district, and ships passing through the Golden Gate. Off to the east side of the hill viewers can take in geographic highlights of San Francisco all the way to the west side of the city: Nob Hill, Telegraph Hill, and the tips of the skyscrapers that dot the downtown financial district.

Russian Hill is one of the city's oldest and most elegant and graceful neighborhoods. Amid stands of tall spruce and cedar trees, this residential area looks and smells like a forest. In keeping with its natural beauty, the city planners built small gardens and narrow walking lanes that wind down the hill through trees and shrubbery. Macondray Lane is a perfect

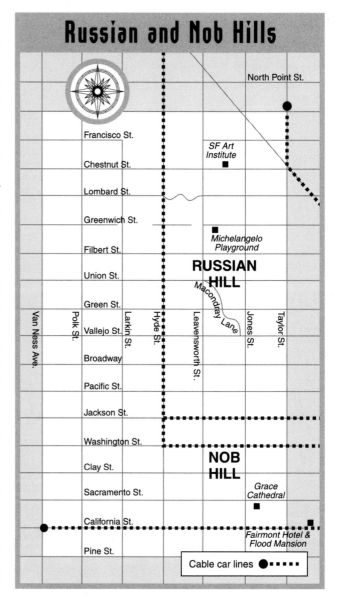

Russian and Nob Hills

North Point St.

Francisco St.

SF Art Institute

Chestnut St.

Lombard St.

Greenwich St.

Michelangelo Playground

Filbert St.

RUSSIAN HILL

Union St.

Macondray Lane

Green St.

Van Ness Ave.

Polk St.

Larkin St.

Hyde St.

Leavenworth St.

Jones St.

Taylor St.

Vallejo St.

Broadway

Pacific St.

Jackson St.

Washington St.

NOB HILL

Clay St.

Grace Cathedral

Sacramento St.

California St.

Fairmont Hotel & Flood Mansion

Pine St.

Cable car lines ●•••••

example. Begin your walk down this lane at the intersection of Vallejo and Jones Streets. As you descend the trails, cement steps, and two flights of wooden stairs, the San Francisco Bay moves in and out of view providing quick glimpses of Alcatraz Island and Marin County.

For one of the more interesting and amusing one-of-a-kind San Francisco experiences, find your way to the crest of Lombard Street. This is the start of the most famous street in San Francisco, known locally as the world's crookedest street. This block-long street is so steep that many years ago city planners designed the street as a series of looping switchbacks that zigzag to the street below. As you either walk or drive down you will meander by ornate million-dollar homes set back along either side of the street. Creative landscaping has turned what could have been a bizarre curiosity into a floral centerpiece. Residents here have learned to accept the fame of their street and the estimated five thousand cars that descend it daily.

Pacific Heights

The fourth recommended hill to investigate is Pacific Heights. Bordered by Bush Street to the south, Lyon Street to the west, Van Ness Avenue to the east, and Union Street to the north, this neighborhood is one of the city's most eclectic.

Stunning views of both the city and the bay can be found here, as they can on the other of the city's hills, but this neighborhood offers more. Unique

Victorian Homes

Part of the San Francisco charm and style includes neighborhoods with restored Victorian homes. The popularity of these wooden homes is the result of the combination of their intricate and detailed design and combinations of vivid and sometimes outlandish colors that distinguishes one from all the others.

Between 1850 and 1900 about fifty thousand Victorian homes were built to accommodate the city's burgeoning population. Many of these houses were lost in the great fire that followed the 1906 earthquake, and others were torn down over the years to make way for new, more modern homes. However, a few thousand of these elegant homes still grace the streets of San Francisco and have become major tourist attractions.

Because the westward spread of the 1906 fire was halted at Van Ness Avenue, the neighborhoods west of that line, especially Pacific Heights, offer the best opportunity for finding these few surviving jewels.

In addition to their fanciful coats of paint, Victorian homes are characterized by several architectural features that distinguish them from other homes in San Francisco. The most notable is their very narrow but long dimension. From the street they are crowded close together, but because they are long and two stories tall, many are spacious inside. Each typically has a prominent and highly decorated front porch reached by a flight of steps, and at least one and often two large windows, called bay windows, facing the street. What makes these bay windows unique is they project out a foot or two on the sides to provide views down to the bay, hence their name. The front of each Victorian also has a variety of decorative wooden details that add unique character and charm.

From the top of Russian Hill, visitors can see Alcatraz, Fisherman's Wharf, and many other San Francisco landmarks.

attractions include row after row of festively and ornately painted turn-of-the-century Victorian houses, the famous Fillmore Auditorium, a collection of old San Francisco mansions that today serve as foreign consulates, sidewalk espresso houses, bookstores, and shops selling hip clothing, records, incense, and other paraphernalia associated with San Francisco's hippie scene.

A casual stroll around the neighborhood will turn up several blocks of restored Victorian homes. Victorian houses are more complicated to build and to paint

Fillmore Auditorium

Fillmore Auditorium—known to most young San Franciscans as the Fillmore, or simply the Aud—is the city's most famous venue for every imaginable type of 1960s music. Every Saturday night for the past few years, one of dozens of groups, many of them local San Francisco bands, have been playing music from jazz and soul to rock and roll. Recently the music everyone comes to hear is called acid rock—rock-and-roll music with sounds and lyrics describing the dreamy and sometimes distorted mental states experienced by people using psychedelic drugs such as LSD, known as acid by nearly everyone who uses it.

The Aud was the brainchild of Bill Graham, a music entrepreneur who bought the thirty-year-old auditorium in 1965 as a place where counterculture music and avant-garde theater presentations appealing to young audiences could be experienced. The first bands to play here, some of which openly flouted the law by advocating the use of marijuana and LSD, received wild ovations by the crowds, while San Francisco parents and the mayor's office tried to close them down.

Friction between the older and younger generations piqued the curiosity of high school and college students who now flock to the Aud to hear increasingly outrageous bands with national reputations play acid-rock music. The music experience is enhanced by coordinated elaborate light shows using strobe lights and colorful spot beams that flash and flicker around the room to create a psychedelic effect, even for those not using drugs.

The Aud has the best that San Francisco can offer for great music. You do not need to use drugs to enjoy the overall excitement of music, dancing, light shows, bizarre clothing, and sometimes bizarre yet entertaining antics of the dancers. Everyone has fun and the Aud has a reputation as a peaceful place where fun seekers can enjoy its friendly atmosphere.

The rock group Cream performs at the Fillmore Auditorium.

than a standard home. Dozens of these Victorian homes standing close together attract tourists and students of architecture to study and marvel at the intricate detail of their wooden, gabled roofs, elegantly crafted porch entryways, and leaded-glass doors and windows. But of greatest attraction are the multihued paint jobs, each a rainbow of carefully matched colors unique to each work of art, which is how these beautiful homes are honored. These remarkably vivid paint jobs have earned the houses the distinction of being called Painted Ladies.

Next wander down to the corner of Geary and Fillmore Streets to the Fillmore Auditorium. This auditorium is home to the most famous and outrageous rock and acid-rock music in America. Since last year the Fillmore has hosted thousands of hip Bay Area music fans who listen to the Grateful Dead, Jefferson Airplane, Carlos Santana, Quicksilver Messenger Service, Janis Joplin,

Moby Grape, the Butterfield Blues Band, and countless other bands that have launched their careers from the Fillmore's stage.

The Saturday night scene inside includes a wild electric light show; high-decibel, raging music; weird scenes of freaky long-haired hipsters wearing garish clothes dancing to the music; and the distinctive odor of marijuana that is openly smoked, even though it is against the law. Guitarist Eric Clapton remembers the Fillmore this way:

There was very much a whole kind of Fillmore energy coming off the audience that combined with the band. When we played the Fillmore for the first time (with the band Cream) the band was in the light show. If you were in the audience, you didn't know who was playing. Not at all. It was a sensory thing.[13]

Chapter 7

Four Distinctive Parks

Far from the raging sounds and psychedelic lights of the Fillmore, San Francisco's many quiet and serene parks provide a much-needed recreational and cultural contrast. Although the city maintains dozens of parks that reflect local needs and interests, four of the larger ones are unusual in their offerings and are of interest to all.

Golden Gate Park

The crown jewel of San Francisco's many parks is Golden Gate Park. The city's largest and most diverse park, this one-thousand-acre recreational area is flanked by Fulton Street on the north and Lincoln Way on the south. Oriented on an east-west axis, it cuts a verdant green swath three miles long and one-half mile wide all the way to the Pacific's surf.

Stretching for more than forty-five city blocks, Golden Gate Park is the city's unofficial playground. This man-made recreational area offers wonderful scenery, including gardens, lakes, and waterfalls, and endless entertainment at the polo field, golf course, archery range, bandstand, and children's playground. Looking at its acres of rolling lawns encircled by more than 1 million trees and plants, miles of shaded horse trails, as well as football, soccer, and baseball fields and lakes makes it difficult to believe that one hundred years ago there was nothing here except endless sand dunes.

Along with its gorgeous green spaces, the park offers numerous cultural attractions, including museums, public art, Sunday concert events, a Victorian conservatory, and restaurants. Although crowded, Sundays are the best days to visit because the main thoroughfares are closed to traffic. The entire park is open to families, athletes, and sun worshippers.

The major museums in the park for both science and the fine arts are the MH de Young Memorial Museum specializing in European and Asian art; the California Academy of Sciences, which includes the Steinhart Aquarium and the Morrison Planetarium, the Asian Art Museum, and the Natural History Museum famed for its geology and paleontology collections.

One of the favorite pleasures located in the park is the oldest public Japanese garden in the nation. It provides winding footpaths, koi pools, an eighteenth-century Japanese statue of Buddha, a Zen rock garden, and a teahouse that serves tea and fortune cookies. The tea garden was built as part of the Midwinter Fair by Makato Hagiwara and his family in 1895. It was here in this lovely serene tea garden that the Hagiwara family first introduced the fortune cookie to the United States.

Golden Gate Park has something for everyone, but a day is hardly enough time to take in all the sights and activities. If hikers manage to ramble all the way to the ocean, they will enjoy a well-deserved rest at the outdoor café at the east entrance to the park. Locating the café is simple; it is in the shadow of the beloved old wooden Dutch windmill. This windmill stands fifty-five feet tall and dominates the area with its four broad wooden arms that once rotated in the wind.

Lincoln Park

Situated on the windswept northeast shoulder of the San Francisco peninsula, this 193-acre parcel of fog-cloaked parkland is one of the city's best kept secrets. Famed for its rare view of the Golden Gate from west of the bridge looking back toward the east, it is a photographer's paradise. Of greater interest to the people of San Francisco is the park's collection of meandering paths that wind along the sheer cliffs overlooking the ocean. These footpaths, intentionally maintained as sim-

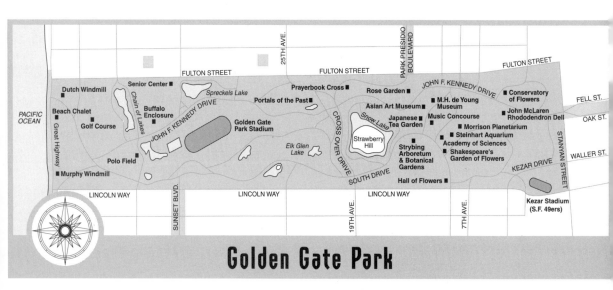

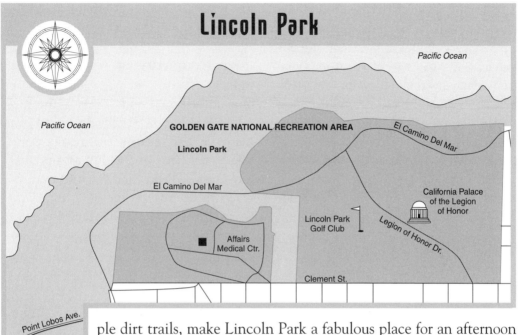

Lincoln Park

Pacific Ocean

Pacific Ocean

GOLDEN GATE NATIONAL RECREATION AREA

Lincoln Park

El Camino Del Mar

El Camino Del Mar

California Palace
of the Legion
of Honor

Lincoln Park
Golf Club

Legion of Honor Dr.

Affairs
Medical Ctr.

Clement St.

Point Lobos Ave.

Cliff House

Upper Great Highway

Ocean Beach Park

Great Highway

ple dirt trails, make Lincoln Park a fabulous place for an afternoon hike or summertime picnic.

At the park's east end is the California Palace of the Legion of Honor museum, which houses a renowned fine-arts collection. The building of the Legion of Honor museum is stunningly picturesque. Set deep within a cypress grove, it is considered by many art aficionados as one of the most beautiful museum settings in the world. Outside the entry, museumgoers are greeted by two life-sized equestrian statues—one of the Spanish conquistador El Cid and the other of the French heroine Joan of Arc. As you enter the expansive entry courtyard, called the Court of Honor, you will pass yet another superb dominating sculpture—*The Thinker*, a work by the nineteenth-century French sculptor August Rodin.

Inside the museum another seventy works of Rodin are displayed in two rooms. The palace's extensive art collection boasts eighty-seven thousand works, most of which are European paintings, sculpture, and decorative arts from the 1300s to the 1900s, as well as art from ancient Assyria, Egypt, Greece, and Rome. The collection is so large that at any one time, museum curators are only able to display about 5 percent of the collection. While here stop into the museum's cafeteria for lunch or a late-afternoon snack where you will be surrounded by a collection of paintings by nineteenth-century French impressionists.

As you depart the museum, make a left at the El Cid statue, cut across the golf course fairway, and descend down the dirt path hugging the side of the cliff. From this little-known spot the lone existing foghorn and lighthouse can be seen and heard. The foghorn is only activated on foggy days, and when you hear it blast its low groan out across the entry of the Golden Gate, you will take home with you an unforgettable memory of San Francisco. This is also a great spot to picnic and lunch while watching freighters silently slip under the Golden Gate Bridge.

The Presidio

Just a short walk from the Legion of Honor museum will take park lovers to the Presidio. Walk down Seacliff Boulevard past many of San Francisco's most elegant stately mansions, and within twenty minutes Presidio Park will come into view.

Almost 120 years ago, in 1846, when the United States declared war

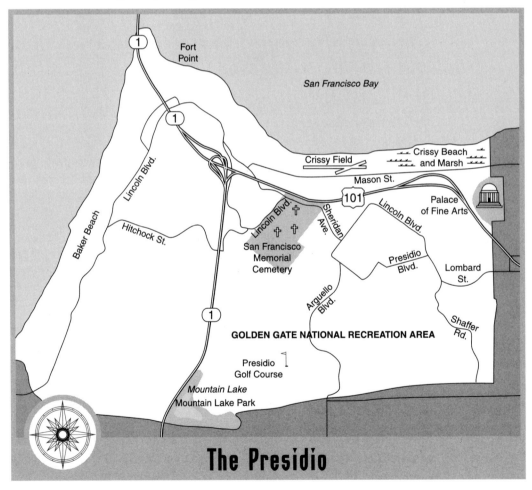

The Presidio

The Japanese Tea Garden

Regarded as the jewel of Golden Gate Park, the Japanese Tea Garden attracts thousands of visitors daily. In the Japanese culture a garden is considered to be one of the highest art forms, expressing in a limited space the essence of nature through the use of specially selected plants, stones, and Japanese art forms. Because tradition holds that evil travels a straight route, the garden has winding paths, offering a serene place to stroll. The Japanese Tea Garden is the type of Japanese garden know as a wet walking garden because of its many ponds and waterfalls.

Owner and designer Makoto Hagiwara constructed the garden, its pavilions, and teahouse, ultimately increasing the size of the garden to about five acres, considerably larger than the original one-acre exhibit. In addition to the landscaping and construction of several structures, Hagiwara imported many plants, bronzes, koi fish, rare Japanese birds, statues of perched and spread-winged eagles, a Shinto shrine, a porcelain lantern, and a wooden Buddha.

Most enjoyed by visitors are the Zen Gardens, representing a modern version of a dry gravel garden—*kare sansu*—symbolizing a miniature mountain scene complete with a stone waterfall and small island surrounded by a gravel river, and the high, arching bridge for walkers that is twice as high as it is long.

against Mexico, the 1,480 wooded acres known as the Presidio was a U.S. military post dedicated to the defense of San Francisco and the Golden Gate. Strategically located, the Presidio occupies the hillside immediately east of the Golden Gate and includes Fort Point located underneath the south end of the Golden Gate Bridge.

This park will provide picnickers and hikers with a very different experience than Golden Gate or Lincoln Parks. As a former military compound Presidio Park is not yet technically a state or national park. Nonetheless the Presidio today is open to the public as a military park and museum. This large expanse of trees, sloping hillsides, grassy knolls, and veterans' cemetery is open to all San Franciscans and the city's visitors. Within the park are historic buildings that predate the Civil War, a collection of coastal defense fortifications, a national cemetery, a historic airfield, a saltwater marsh, forests, beaches, native plant habitats, coastal bluffs, miles of hiking and biking, and some of the most spectacular vistas in the Bay Area.

Take a hike down one of many dirt trails to the cemetery. A small number of gravestones date back to the Civil War, a handful to World War I, and the vast majority to World War II. From here wander down to the water's edge immediately under the south end of the Golden Gate

Bridge. Here, open to the public, you will discover one of the many secrets of San Francisco—Fort Point.

This brick fortification, now speckled with orange paint from painting crews touching up the Golden Gate Bridge, is the oldest military fort in the West. Between 1853 and 1861 the U.S. Army Corps of Engineers constructed Fort Point to protect the entry of the bay with a battery of cannons. Wander in at no charge and take a tour of the fort, its cannons, soldiers' facilities and storerooms, and an unobstructed view of the Golden Gate.

Ocean Beach Park

San Francisco's beaches along the Pacific Ocean can be a great place to enjoy the sun, family entertainment, and a variety of water sports during the summer months. One of the favorite oceanfront parks in the city is Ocean Beach Park that runs the six-mile length of the western edge of San Francisco. On the warmest days San Franciscans congregate here to exercise and

Once a military compound, San Francisco's Presidio is today a lush park that welcomes countless visitors every year.

Steinhart Aquarium

The Steinhart Aquarium houses the largest collection of marine life on the West Coast.

One of the great activities in Golden Gate Park that will not cost you a dime is a visit to Steinhart Aquarium. This place has one of the most intriguing entrances of any aquarium. As you enter an enormous foyer, straight ahead is the aquarium's famous alligator pit in which a dozen alligators sleep on rocks and lazily glide through shallow water. A waterfall covered with ferns and a variety of aquatic plants provides a refreshing backdrop. Surrounding the alligator pit is the aquarium's small yet exotic collection of reptiles.

The main attraction, the large fish collection, is in separate rooms to the left and right of the alligator pit. The Steinhart Aquarium houses the largest collection of fish on the West Coast. A dozen rooms house more than one hundred individual tanks exhibiting more than five thousand aquatic animals in a variety of diverse underwater environments. Six hundred species of fish live here, along with many small marine mammals and amphibians and a collection of black-footed penguins.

Fort Point

Fort Point is one of the easiest places in San Francisco to locate; simply find the Golden Gate Bridge. The fort sits directly under the south end of the bridge down at the water's edge. As you enter the fort's inner courtyard, you will see the three tiers of cannon ports well protected behind thirty-foot-thick brick walls. Although most of the original cannons have been removed, three remain for historical purposes, along with many other fascinating military memorabilia.

Back in the days of the gold rush, that also coincided with the expulsion of Mexico from California, an American military commission determined that the San Francisco Bay needed a solid defense. The recommendation was to position a fort on the south side of the Golden Gate with a battery of heavy cannons. With only 1.2 miles of water to be defended, military strategists speculated that any enemy ship attempting to run through the gate would encounter a deadly barrage of cannon fire from the fort's 126 massive cannons. The site became known as Fort Point.

Fort Point never fired a single cannonball at an enemy ship, and by 1900 the fort was declared obsolete. When initial plans were drawn for the Golden Gate Bridge in the early 1930s, engineers recommended destroying the antiquated fort. Local historians and community groups, however, who favored preserving it, triumphed. Because of their victory you can now stand on the site and crane your head straight up to see the bridge's steel arch that supports the roadway as it passes over the fort. As the excessive paint splatter covering the fort suggests, this is not a good place to visit when the bridge's paint crew is at work overhead.

enjoy surfboarding, body surfing, surf fishing, and swimming.

This beach has many other offerings in addition to water sports. Parts of the beach reveal tide pools at low tide where nature lovers can explore the tide-pool life of crabs, sea urchins, sea stars, abalone, eels, and a variety of small rock fish. Along one section near Fort Funston, where a stretch of high bluffs looms up, hang gliders catch warm air currents to soar over the beach and waves. Another favorite spot for San Franciscans where Golden Gate Park meets the beach is Playland-at-the-Beach. This is the city's only year-round amusement park complete with rollercoaster rides, hamburger and hot-dog stands, a mystery house, and a variety of novelty shops.

Chapter 8

Day Trips Outside San Francisco

San Francisco may be the undisputed hub of all cultural and financial activities in the Bay Area, yet many of the towns and cities around the perimeter of the bay provide their own unique cultural, historic, and geographic attractions. There are many to choose from, and whichever one or more you choose, each will provide a refreshing break from the busy and often noisy streets of San Francisco.

The closest and easiest to reach is Marin County, immediately north of San Francisco.

Marin County

Across the Golden Gate Bridge from San Francisco, Marin County is a region with some of the most breathtaking scenic beauty that can be found anywhere. It is a laid-back and tuned-in cluster of quaint bayside, upscale, chic communities. When it comes to trendy living, whether it is the recent hot tub craze, Eastern meditation, bicycling, or fondue parties, residents of Marin County are doing it before it becomes the rage.

Once you are across the Golden Gate Bridge and pass through a short tunnel, Highway 101 forks. Off to the left Highway 1 branches off and heads to the rugged coast by way of primeval forests of towering redwoods. Off to the right you can find your way to the charming bayside city of Sausalito, home of enchanting restaurants, art galleries, and million-dollar houseboats. Some of these restaurants float directly over the water, providing serene and unusual dining.

If you are looking for a day of shopping and a relaxing lunch on the wharf with a dazzling view of the San Francisco skyline, Sausalito is the place for you. The city's shops are all down the hill along the bay on one small street that is the commercial artery for the city.

The picturesque bayside city of Sausalito is home to a number of elegant shops, upscale restaurants, and million-dollar homes.

One unusual attraction known only to the locals, which is definitely worth a visit, is the model of the bay. This scale model is housed in a two-acre warehouse owned by the National Geodetic Survey. Inside, at no cost, visitors will see a working scale model of the bay, which is used by scientists to test the effects of drought, floods, landfill, and other changes.

If you took the left turn and headed for the coast, you are in for a magnificent day of hiking and exploring. The wild Pacific coastline stretches north to Stinson Beach, Bolinas, and the fog-swept Point Reyes National Seashore. There remote spots are great for whale watching, collecting shells and drift-

wood, and finding the occasional petrified whale bones. A bit farther north up the coast, a hike up the twenty-six-hundred-foot Mount Tamalpais accords a breathtaking 360-degree panorama of the ocean, the bay, San Francisco, and all three major bridges. Mount Tamalpais also overlooks the picturesque stand of redwoods in Muir Woods State Park. Here two hundred miles of hiking and biking trails wind around the mountain, and deer, fox, bobcat, and even the occasional mountain lion dwell in the forests and meadows.

Gold Country

California's Gold Country is just a short drive northeast of Sacramento. This en-

Head Shops

Head shops are a phenomenon found primarily in Haight-Ashbury and on Telegraph Avenue in Berkeley. Also commonly called psychedelic shops, they are small retail shops that cater to hippies and specifically to the drug component of the hippie culture. The name *head shop* comes from the term *drug head,* a commonly used term describing full-time drug users. Several head shops can be found on Telegraph that stock an amazing collection of trendy, hippie stuff and drug paraphernalia.

One of the classic head shops on Telegraph is Xanadu. Enter through its curtain of beads and you will encounter colorful tie-dyed shirts and skirts, beaded leather vests, feathered headbands, and leather sandals. The biggest sellers are blue jeans embroidered with peace signs, sun flowers, and the unmistakable outline of the distinctive marijuana leaf.

Hanging from the walls are psychedelic posters of rock musicians. Especially popular are singers Jim Morrison, Bob Dylan, and Janis Joplin, and guitarist Jimi Hendrix. Also favored are posters of drug gurus such as poet Allen Ginsberg and LSD proponent Timothy Leary.

It is the drug paraphernalia that makes head shops unique, however. Particularly popular are the wide variety of pipes used to smoke marijuana. The hot marijuana smoke can burn the lining of the lungs, so head shops specialize in pipes that cool the smoke. Most popular are water pipes—called bongs or hookahs—that draw the hot smoke through a bowl of cool water before it is inhaled.

Posters cover the walls and ceiling of this Haight-Ashbury head shop.

tire region is often referred to as the Mother Lode because of its incredibly rich vein of gold stretching 120 miles from Bear Valley to Auburn. The name gradually came to encompass the entire gold-rich Sierra Nevada foothills region. Historical records list more than five hundred mining camps and diggings from the gold rush era. Three hundred have disappeared without a trace, but a few remain either as busy towns or quiet little hamlets. Try splitting a day between Nevada City and Grass Valley.

Between Grass Valley and Nevada City, the Empire Mine has recently been made into a state historical monument that provides tours of one of California's largest and most productive gold mines. It operated between 1850 and 1956, producing close to 6 million ounces of pure gold. Park rangers will take visitors on a tour of the facilities that includes entering the main shaft leading to 367 miles of abandoned, flooded tunnels one mile below the surface. Next on the tour are the massive hydraulic crushers that crushed the gold-bearing quartz rock into pieces the size of grains of sand. Next, visitors will see the washbox where the quartz and gold were washed with water before heading by conveyor belt to the refinery where the gold was separated from the quartz. Here, in a carefully ventilated and guarded room, the crushed rock was washed over copper cables coated with mercury. Since gold will adhere to the mercury, at the end of the day mine operators scraped the mercury and gold from the cables. Next they heated the amalgam, causing the mercury to vaporize leaving behind a lump of pure gold. Each ton of crushed granite removed from the mine yielded one ounce of gold.

After a tour of the mine, head for historic Nevada City. The main street here has been restored to reflect the shops and businesses one would have found one hundred years ago. The street is narrow and all of the stores are wooden, facing onto a narrow sidewalk. Through this city, high up in the pines of the Sierra foothills, a picturesque river meanders as it flows down the hill.

If there is time, travel just south of Nevada City to the city of Colma where the first gold strike was made by John Sutter in 1848. And only a few miles from there, a railroad museum in Auburn displays many artifacts from the transcontinental railroad that the Chinese hammered and blasted through the mountains back in 1863.

A walk through these mining buildings is just one of the stops visitors make on their tour of the Empire Mine.

Lake Tahoe

Next on the list of recommended destinations, just an hour's drive farther east, high in the Sierra mountain range, is Lake Tahoe, one of the nation's most pristine lakes. Lake Tahoe is a favorite recreational haven for many San Franciscans because of its great depth, water clarity, and beautiful alpine surroundings. Resting at an unusually high elevation for a lake, Tahoe sits on the border of California and Nevada. With an average surface elevation of 6,225 feet above sea level, Lake Tahoe is the highest major lake in the United States. Its average depth is slightly more than one thousand feet, which is second only to Oregon's Crater Lake. The water temperature is brisk yet attractive year round and draws sightseers, boaters, and

swimmers. Far from any large city or sources of pollution, the lake has maintained its crystal-clear waters that provide swimmers more than one hundred feet of underwater visibility.

Roughly twenty-two miles long by twelve miles wide, the lake's seventy-two miles of shoreline provide summer visitors with a variety of water sports. Favorite summer activities are swimming, boating, fishing, and waterskiing. The high mountain peaks surrounding the lake, several of which exceed the ten-thousand-foot range, provide additional outdoor recreation for hikers, campers, horseback riders, and bicyclists.

When the seasons change and winter snows cover the mountains, Tahoe becomes an equally popular destination for skiers. Several of California's best ski resorts are located within a few miles of Tahoe, including Squaw Valley, home of the 1960 Winter Olympics. In addition to several downhill ski slopes, this alpine setting provides hundreds of miles of trails through dense pine and cedar forests for cross-country skiers.

A few miles from Tahoe is Donner Summit. Students of American history come here to pay their respects to the Donner Party, a hardy and intrepid group of pioneers that attempted to cross through Donner Pass in 1846. At an elevation of seven thousand feet, these pioneers struggling to make their way over

The magnificent Half Dome looms above the trees in Yosemite National Park.

the Sierras became hopelessly stranded and lost in a winter snowstorm. Diaries found among the dead told grisly tales of cannibalism as survivors ate the dead to trying to hold out until a search party could locate them.

Yosemite National Park

High in the rugged Sierra Nevada mountain range sits Yosemite National Park, the most visited park in America. Earthquakes, glaciers, and other forces of nature over millions of years sliced, warped, and compressed the landscape to create towering granite cliffs, thundering waterfalls, steep mountains, and deep alpine lakes. In 1890, John Muir, naturalist and Sierra Club founder, called it "a landscape . . . that after all my wanderings still appears as the most beautiful I have ever beheld."[14]

Since then millions of visitors annually have explored, climbed, photographed, and experienced the park's grandeur. Driving beside the winding, cool Merced River, the banks of which are decorated by thick, blossoming dogwood; deeply cracked bark of ponderosa and sugar pine; and thickets of low manzanita brush; El Capitan looms off to the left. The largest monolith in the world, this gigantic granite spire, with a sheer drop to the valley floor of almost thirty-six hundred feet, attracts only the most experienced rock climbers. Stop for a moment to watch climbers rope their way up the face. Most will take two to five days to make the climb, depending upon experience.

Another three miles ahead looms Half Dome. As its name suggests it was once a dome, but long ago—geologists do not know when—a deep fissure weakened, releasing half of the dome to crash to the floor below. Geologists and acoustical engineers speculate that the sound of the crash could have been heard as far away as San Francisco had anyone been living there at the time. Not far from Half Dome is the equally dramatic Yosemite Falls, the third-highest waterfall in the world. The falls drop twenty-eight hundred feet in two stages to the valley below. The hike to the top is a strenuous 6.6-mile round trip, but the views of the valley below make the hike worthwhile.

In addition to the natural wonders of the park are the many amenities in the valley. Lodges, cabins, and campsites are available, as are restaurants, stables, the Ansel Adams photographic museum, general stores, and public trams that carry visitors through the park at no cost. One of the best ways to see parts of Yosemite that will provide a lifetime of memories is renting bicycles and riding along the valley floor. Park rangers have built bike paths over stone bridges, across grassy meadows grazed by deer, and across streambeds dry during the summer but occasionally swollen with the ice-cold spring thaw.

Climbing Half Dome

Every year 4 million people visit Yosemite Valley, and every one of them sees Half Dome, Yosemite's most famous landmark. A very small percentage of them consider hiking to the top and, of those, an even smaller percentage actually does it. Its name aptly describes this great granite half-domed monolith, and the climb to the top is legendary. Each year, dozens of skilled rock climbers rope their way up the sheer face to the top, while a few thousand intrepid hikers take the longer yet not as dangerous sixteen-mile hike up the back side of the dome.

Do not think this hike is a piece of cake. The first ten miles pass Vernal and then Nevada Falls, both extraordinarily beautiful thundering waterfalls spraying welcome ice-cold mists on the faces of resolute hikers. The last two miles are up steep, jagged chunks of granite that reflect the hot sun. The last leg of one thousand feet is nearly straight up—a 70 percent angle—that can be accomplished only with the assistance of hand cables drilled into the rock that climbers use to pull their way to the summit. Once you are on top, the awe-inspiring view of the valley below makes it all worthwhile. When you return to the valley, you have a legitimate right to buy a T-shirt with the outline of Half Dome proudly proclaiming: "I MADE IT TO THE TOP."

Berkeley

Berkeley is precisely due east of the Golden Gate Bridge. A relatively small city with a population of 120,000, it is principally known as the home of the University of California. The academic reputation of the university, campus landmarks, and the recent influx of carefree hippies who are welcomed by the student population have made Berkeley the second-most-popular tourist stop of the bay cities.

As visitors drive up University Avenue they will find themselves at the east entry to the campus. A drive across the picturesque campus takes you past libraries, laboratories, classrooms, monuments, and tree-lined Strawberry Creek that meanders through manicured, rolling lawns where statues of famous faculty stand bearing Latin and Greek inscriptions.

The most dominant and photographed landmark is Sather Tower, more commonly called the Campanile. This 314-foot-high marble bell tower modeled after the one at St. Mark's square in Venice, Italy, has a carillon of forty-eight bells that is played daily at noon. For a mere ten cents, the same price it cost when the tower opened in 1914, visitors are welcome to ride the tiny elevator to the top, where a spectacular panoramic view of the campus below and San Francisco on the horizon makes the claustrophobic ride worthwhile.

Immediately up the hill from the Campanile is the Lawrence

Hall of Science, named after E.O. Lawrence, inventor of the cyclotron used by physicists to accelerate subatomic particles close to the speed of light. The museum here, built for junior high and high school students, is filled with physics memorabilia, interactive experiments for students, and a room displaying Lawrence's Nobel Prize which he received for his discovery in 1939. The university is famous for its faculty, which includes more

A short elevator ride to the top of Sather Tower provides a breathtaking view of the University of California at Berkeley campus.

Nobel Prize laureates than any other American university.

Next door to the Lawrence Hall of Science is the the cyclotron, which provides visitors a limited tour. The cyclotron is a 184-inch-diameter circle that magnetically accelerates subatomic particles close to the speed of light to study their component parts. Although no one is permitted inside the actual ring where the particles are accelerated, visitors can see the control room, the massive concrete blocks used as insulators, and displays celebrating the discovery of many rare elements. Element number 97, for example, was discovered here and named berkelium after Berkeley; number 99, einsteinium, was named after physicist Albert Einstein; and element 103, lawrencium, was named for E.O. Lawrence.

The Ave.

If you really want to experience eccentric behavior that you probably will not find at home, wander over to the south side of campus to Telegraph Avenue—affectionately known to students and faculty as simply Tele or The Ave. Telegraph Avenue is the center of Berkeley's colorful student zone filled with some of the best rock and classical music stores in the country, great used hippie clothing stores, more excellent new and used bookstores than anywhere else in America, and countless restaurants and coffeehouses offering cups of frothy cappuccino and strong espresso. Some of these coffeehouses, such as the Mediterraneum, Florentine, and Forum, double as popular music spots. You will also find lively street performers, and vendors selling clothing, jewelry, pottery, water pipes, and various other hippie arts and crafts. Be aware that many of the panhandling hipsters asking if you have "any spare change" are often the children of well-off university faculty. Stop a moment to listen to the many street-corner proselytizers espousing political and social opinions from the far left to the far right. Whatever your political inclination might be, Telegraph is a must-see neighborhood if you are exploring the treasures of Berkeley and want to catch a glimpse of what gives this city its wonderfully eccentric reputation.

A visit to Berkeley is a fitting end to a visit to San Francisco because in many respects it is a microcosm of the larger city. Both cities enjoy and cultivate a reputation for embracing revolutionary thinkers, promoting bookstores catering to unorthodox and international writers, supporting the hippie lifestyle, embracing the arts, and encouraging all forms of free expression. On your return to San Francisco across the Bay Bridge, take a moment to enjoy one last view of the city's famous hills, the Golden Gate Bridge, the many islands in the bay, the Ferry Building, Sausalito, and the tour boats that weave their way among the many sailboats that dot the bay.

Notes

Introduction: The City
1. Quoted in *Tripadvisor*, "San Francisco," 2003. www.tripadvisor.com.
2. Quoted in *S.F. Heart*, "San Francisco Quotes," 2002. www.sfheart.com.

Chapter One: The History of San Francisco
3. Miguel Costansó, *The Discovery of San Francisco Bay: The Portolá Expedition: The Diary of Miguel Costansó*, ed. Peter Browning. Lafayette, CA: Great West Books, 1992, p. 119.
4. Quoted in *Museum of the City of San Francisco*, "The Discovery of Gold in California." www.sfmuseum.org.
5. John A. Martini, *Fortress Alcatraz*. Kailua, HI: Pacific Monograph, 1990, p. 15.
6. Quoted in *S.F. Heart*, "The Fall of San Francisco: Some Personal Observations," 2002. www.sfheart.com.

Chapter Three: First Day, Getting to Know the City
7. Quoted in *S.F. Heart*, "San Francisco Quotes."
8. Quoted in *S.F. Heart*, "San Francisco Quotes."

9. Quoted in *S.F. Heart*, "San Francisco Quotes."

Chapter Four: Five Classic Explorations
10. Joe David Brown, *The Hippies: Who They Are, Where They Are, Why They Act That Way, How They May Affect Our Society*. New York: Time, 1967, p. 1.

Chapter Five: Four Unforgettable Walks
11. Quoted in Heidi Benson, et al., "City Lights and the Counterculture," *SF gate.com*, 2003. www. sfgate.com.

Chapter Six: Four Hills of Distinction
12. Quoted in Christopher P. Verplanck, "Telegraph Hill," *San Francisco Apartment Association*, September 2002. www.sfaa.org.
13. Quoted in *Fillmore*, "Fillmore History," 2001. www.thefillmore.com.

Chapter Eight: Day Trips Outside San Francisco
14. Quoted in "Yosemite—A National Treasure," *YosemitePark.com*, 2003. www.yosemitepark.com.

For Further Reading

Sherri Gavan, *The Hippies of the Haight*. St. Louis, MO: New Critics Press, 1972. The author presents excellent observations of hippie behavior and drug use.

Tro Harper, *Nowhere Except San Francisco: Memoirs of a Resident Tourist*. Kentwood, CA: Oak Point Press, 1999. This book reflects Harper's years as a San Francisco journalist and bookseller. Beginning with the 1950s and carrying through to the 1990s, Harper discusses the life and energy of the city generally and explores its icons in detail.

George Perry, *San Francisco in the Sixties*. London: Pavilion Press, 2001. The author describes the 1960s as one of San Francisco's most crucial decades. Perry focuses on what he perceives to be an era of unprecedented social and cultural revolution. He describes the collapse of old cultural barriers replaced with new freedoms and an explosion of creative energy expressed in the arts, fashion, politics, and lifestyles.

Rand Richards, *Historic San Francisco: A Concise History and Guide*.Essex, UK: Heritage, 1991. The author provides a lively historic narrative of San Francisco from its very beginnings all the way through to the earthquake of 1989. He provides historic insights into buildings, sites, museums, parks, and the usual tourist traps, while devoting a chapter to cultural San Francisco during the decades of the 1950s and 1960s.

Tom Wolfe, *The Electric Kool-Aid Acid Test*. New York: Farrar, Straus & Giroux, 1987. This is a novel written in 1967 chronicling novelist Ken Kesey and his band of Merry Pranksters. In 1966 Kesey led a group of psychedelic sympathizers around the country in a painted bus, presiding over LSD-induced "acid tests" all along the way. This is considered one of the greatest books about the cultural history of the 1960s and the hippies.

Works Consulted

Books

Joe David Brown, *The Hippies: Who They Are, Where They Are, Why They Act That Way, How They May Affect Our Society*. New York: Time, 1967. This insightful study of the hippies discusses the movement, its evolution, its attraction for adolescents, its subculture of drugs, and its communal lifestyle.

Miguel Costansó, *The Discovery of San Francisco Bay: The Portolá Expedition: The Diary of Miguel Costansó*. Ed. Peter Browning. Lafayette, CA: Great West Books, 1992. This diary, in both English and Spanish, is fascinating reading for the early history of California.

John A. Martini, *Fortress Alcatraz*. Kailua, HI: Pacific Monograph, 1990. Martini's work spans the entire history of Alcatraz but focuses on the period between 1848 and 1934, when it functioned as a military prison. Martini provides a masterful profile of the early fortifications and armament, complete with photographs and maps. This is a thorough discussion of Alcatraz as a military fort and prison.

Czeslaw Milosz, *Visions from San Francisco Bay*. New York: Farrar, Straus & Giroux, 1983. Written in Berkeley during the unrest of 1968, this is a series of essays about the student revolts and hippie movement in the Bay Area. Because the author is Polish, the essays uniquely express very different views.

Bill Morgan, *The Beat Generation in San Francisco: A Literary Tour*. San Francisco: City Lights Books, 2003. Morgan presents a blow-by-blow account of the places where the beat writers lived, wrote, and published their stories and poems.

James W. Schock, *The Bridge: A Celebration*. Mill Valley, CA: Golden Gate International, 1997. Schock's book includes some technical discussions, material on the opening-day celebration, excellent photographs, and an informative year-by-year history.

Internet Sources

Heidi Benson et al., "City Lights and the Counterculture," *SF gate.com*, 2003. www.sfgate.com.

Allen Cohen, "Additional Notes on the S.F. Oracle," *Rockument: Rock Music History*, 2002. www.rockument.com.

College of Letters and Science, "The Class of 1928 Carillon: A Brief History," UC Berkeley, 2002. www.ls.berkeley.edu.

Fillmore, "Fillmore History," 2001. www.thefillmore.com.

Robert Hass, "City Lights and the Counterculture," *SFgate.com*, September 2002. www.sfgate.com.

Josh Merlin, "City Lights Book Store 50th Anniversary 1953–2003," *SFSTATION.COM*, 2003. www.sfstation.com.

Museum of the City of San Francisco, "The Discovery of Gold in California." www.sfmuseum.org.

George Riser, "1967," *University of Virginia Library*, 2002. www.lib.virginia.edu.

S.F. Heart, "The Fall of San Francisco: Some Personal Observations," 2002. www.sfheart.com

———, "San Francisco Quotes," 2002. www.sfheart.com.

ThinkExist.com, "William Saroyan." 2002, www.thinkexist.com.

Tripadvisor, "San Francisco," 2003. www.tripadvisor.com.

Bill Urlaub, "America's Only Literary Landmark," *Guardsman Online*, City College of San Francisco, 2001. www.theguardsman.com.

Christopher P. Verplanck, "Telegraph Hill," *San Francisco Apartment Association*, September 2002. www.sfaa.org.

YosemitePark.com, "Yosemite—A National Treasure," 2003. www.yosemitepark.com.

Websites

Heart of the City (www.mistersf.com). This website serves as an excellent tour guide to many of San Francisco's most well-known tourist attractions. It provides photographs accompanied by lively text.

Virtual Museum of the City of San Francisco (www.sfmuseum.org). This website provides an excellent history of San Francisco with highlights describing in detail a dozen of the most important moments in the city's history. Each era is documented by photographs, newspaper articles, and excerpts from diaries.

Index